T0148085

CONQUERING CALYPSO

WHEN THE ANSWER IS CANCER

LAURA JANCA

Order this book online at www.trafford.com
or email orders@trafford.com

Most Trafford titles are also available at major online book retailers.

Printed in the United States of America.

ISBN: 978-1-4907-5254-9 (sc)
ISBN: 978-1-4907-5253-2 (e)

Trafford rev. 12/18/2014

www.trafford.com
North America & international
toll-free: 1 888 232 4444 (USA & Canada)
fax: 812 355 4082

 # Dedication

I would like to dedicate this book to the following:

To my BED team: Bobbie Rupp, Eva Richardson and Dawn Sommers, and to my BFF of more than thirty years Kelly Estes. I cannot imagine how hard this journey would have been without you!

To Jim DiNapoli, may he rest in peace. He taught me so much and showed me a very different way to look at life. He also showed me love and brought wonderful people into my life.

 # Acknowledgements

I would like to thank the many, many friends and family who showed me support in so many ways during this journey. From the moment I first heard the word cancer my friends and family rallied around me and made sure I knew that I would not be walking this journey alone.

From the countless cards and letters, gifts sent from afar, rides to chemo, shoulders to cry on and ears to listen, my friends and family were there for me.

I am reminded of the "Footprints" poem as I know for certain that there was just one set of footprints during this period of my life.

My medical team was absolutely superior. I'd like to give an extra special thanks to the following:

Gregory Liebscher, MD, FACS and all the staff

Uchenna Njiaju, MD Oncology
Rose Gates, NP, PhD Oncology and all the staff

In addition, a great big thank you to:
Elaine Hubler, LPC, LAC, PC
Elizabeth Roberts, Whole Foods Chef & Nutritionist

 # Introduction

So, you've picked up this book most likely because you asked yourself "What is Calypso and why is she standing on a mountain?"

These are some definitions of Calypso:

Greek Mythology: A sea nymph who delayed Odysseus on her island, Ogygia, for seven years.

A type of music that originated in the West Indies, notably in Trinidad, and is characterized by improvised lyrics on topical or broadly humorous subjects.

A terrestrial orchid (Calypso bulbosa) native to northern temperate regions, having a rose-pink flower with an inflated pouchlike lip usually marked with white, purple, and yellow.

My definition however, is much different. I am not a sea nymph nor have I ever kept anyone on my island. I don't even have an island (yet). I do like the Calypso music. I've never seen the orchid Calypso but it sounds pretty.

Calypso is the word I use for cancer. See, a funny thing happened on the way to "the rest of my life." I was detained by breast cancer. Except I didn't like that word, so I called it Calypso. It wasn't about being held on an island for seven years. This was a period of about one year in the mountains from the time I was diagnosed with breast cancer until my final surgery almost one year later.

What makes my book different? For starters, I never thought of this as a bad thing. I actually think this journey was a blessing in many ways. I had six surgeries and sixteen rounds of chemotherapy over six months, and I was hospitalized with a staph infection for five days. The thing is, none of it was as horrible as most people think. The surgeries were fairly easy and uncomplicated. I might add they were very quick too (for me that is)!

Chemo was actually an adventure and at times dare I say fun? I had different people take me each time so they could share the experience with me. I thought it was very interesting and felt obligated to educate any of my friends that were kind enough to escort me!

Yes, some of this is typical for cancer patients. However, I feel I must tell you that also during this year while I was doing surgeries, chemo and numerous doctor appointments I also made time to hike, zip-line, rock climb, tube down the river and ride a bike 19 miles down from the top of Pikes Peak.

You know what they say: "When the going gets tough, the tough get going." I was determined not to let a little Calypso interfere with my life!

In the end, I feel I truly have an abundant life. Over the course of this year I had friends near and far rally around me. I was quite overwhelmed at times with love and support.

So, my hope is that this book will help someone in a similar situation. Whether it be Calypso you are dealing with or some other health related (or non-health related) issue, keeping things in perspective is crucial to survival. That and a good sense of humor! I hope there is something in this book for everyone. There is even plenty of boob-talk for the guys!

I wake each day with gratitude for having had this opportunity to feel love like I've never known and to learn what is really important in life – the people that you share it with. And so I hope you will take this journey with me now as well.

# A few words from the support team:

"If someone had told me a year ago that my sister Laura would be diagnosed with breast cancer, I would have thought they were crazy. I mean, except for a slight chocolate addiction and elevated blood pressure, Laura was the picture of good health. But first there was the "I found a lump" conversation, then the dreaded phone call with the biopsy results a few weeks later. Yes, the answer was cancer. The weeks and months that followed were the most difficult that my sister had ever faced in her life, but she was more than up to the challenge and displayed more courage, grace, strength, and humor than I thought was humanly possible. I love and admire her more than words can say for the way she handled herself throughout her journey. The complaints were rare, though I know she shed a tear or two when she was alone. If you or a loved one is faced with a similar journey, I encourage you to read this book. You'll laugh at times and cry at times, but mostly you'll be inspired by the quiet strength and sense of hope that my sister carried with her throughout her battle with (and ultimate victory over) breast cancer."
- Eva Richardson

"Laura is a shining example of what a positive attitude, healthy living and fresh air will do for you. Cancer does not stand a chance, when you continue to live and love through the tough stuff."
-Bobbie Rupp

"When my dear friend Laura was diagnosed with cancer we were all shocked. I lost my aunt to breast cancer 16 years ago. I never went to see her when she was fighting it since I was sure she would overcome it. She didn't survive and I've lived with that guilt since. I wasn't going to let the opportunity pass by again to help someone that I cared for. Laura is such a fighter and has such a positive attitude that we knew she would kick cancer's butt. She had many more good days than bad. I think it took more of an emotional toll on her than a physical toll. Being her close friend made it hard to watch her go through it at times. However, I'm glad she chose me to be there and would do it all over again. You'll love her humorous and down to earth story of conquering Calypso!"
-Dawn Sommers

"How can I possibly begin to describe what it's like when you get that call "Kelly I found a lump." My heart sank! NO! Not Laura! Not my friend - not the person who is the other part of me! We've been through so much together in the last 33 years. We could do without this but the choice was not ours. It seems strange to think that was over a year ago now. So many ups and downs and so much learned. Those who experience this type of thing learn a lot about illness, pain, drugs, regrets and even death. Laura not only learned all of this and overcame it, she learned how to live. How to truly LIVE! Her illness did not define her. Her strength and courage did!"
-Kelly Estes

My Story

This story covers a period in my life for about a year. It was quite an extraordinary year though. This was a year that changed my life and who I am, what I hoped for the future and how I look at life. You see, when something threatens your life it also changes your life. I have had a very nice life up until this point… no complaints really. But that's just it. My life had become somewhat stagnant. I might even say it was boring, at least to me. Of course that's when things tend to get shaken apart for I know God has a great sense of humor. I don't mind that really because I trust the path that I am on which leaves me one choice in the matter… to laugh along with Him.

This is my story and journal of my experience with breast cancer. I started journaling about it shortly after I was diagnosed knowing that this journey was going to be a long one.

My story isn't all that extraordinary and there may be similar stories from others like me. I guess the difference for me is that I kept a positive attitude, had a great support team and even found humor throughout the journey. The doctors and nurses all say that's 90% of winning the battle right there.

My battle has come to an end and I refuse to be defined by what I've been through. To the world I am a survivor. I prefer to think I of myself as an "Overcomer." This wasn't a life occurrence that left me asking "why me?" I knew all along that there was a reason for this. I wasn't sure at the time what that reason was and I'm not completely sure even now. However, I believe it was a wake up call. I can easily go back to the life I was living and I'm sure everything would be just fine. But maybe… just maybe, there is something bigger and better waiting out there for me. That's what I believe and I am at a point in my life now, after this journey where I am taking a "leap of faith" to see what that something might be.

And so, if you will, take this journey with me. Cancer isn't always a bad thing… and chemo, well you can choose to kick its butt as I did. Everyone deals with these matters in their own way. I made up my mind to stay strong and "fight like a girl!"

If this story helps just one person, then it will have been worth it.

Okay, two other things that would make it worth it for me… being on the Ellen show and getting an interview by Matt Lauer on the Today Show would be very cool! I've dreamt of that for a long time so it would be great to check that off the bucket list!

Conquering Calypso

October 17, 2013: Celebrating 55years of ME!

I just celebrated birthday number 55 with about as many friends and life is good.

The thing is, the older I get the more I think about life in general and more specifically my own life and how it stacks up. I find myself pondering the question of "why am I here?" I suppose that's normal for us "over 50 folks."

Is this truly the "speed limit" of my life? Am I on the right path? Am I prepared for the next 10-20 years and beyond? Retirement is merely 10-15 years away... then what? Oh yeah... more time to hike and spend outdoors in Colorado! The thing about pondering what your life is about and asking all of these questions is that… you may get answers in ways you never expected.

October 26: A speed bump….
Nine days after this birthday I discovered a lump in my left breast. In a week whirlwind, I get in to see my doctor, who writes up an order for a diagnostic mammogram and ultrasound. I tell myself "it's just a cyst."

Two days later, that's done but it only shows that it is not a cyst, so the following day I am scheduled for a biopsy. They not only found and biopsied the mass but found a smaller one in the lymph node. This isn't looking good but I tell myself "it's just a benign tumor."

November 6: The Rumor of a Tumor? No, The answer is cancer….
And a mere six days later I get a call from the doctor. It's not a benign tumor. That word that I did not want to hear is spoken…Cancer. Why couldn't they call it Calypso or Kaleidoscope or Coco Puffs? Just something that doesn't sound so dreadful. Of course, whatever they called it, then that word would be the word that sounds dreadful. Still, I think I will refer to it from here on out as Calypso. My case of Calypso doesn't sound so bad now does it?

In any case, I just received this news not even an hour ago and immediately began making phone calls. The first call is to my BFF Kelly, then to my mom. That was a good order to proceed because the first time I had to say "I have Calypso," I choked. Kelly understands this but I wanted to be brave and strong when I talked to my mom. Probably because she has always been brave and strong in the time of any crisis our family has endured.

So, on to the phone calls…the more I make the easier it gets to say the words. Some might say I am just in denial or that I haven't processed it yet. I'm not sure but I really feel okay with this. I have had a few sleepless nights while waiting for the results and the words Kelly said to me keep circling back… "It's going to be okay, no matter what."

I saw something posted online the other day that spoke of moments of darkness and that's when it's just you and God. Something about that just brings me to a peaceful place. I have always said that God doesn't give us more than we can handle, so obviously He knows I can handle this… and now I know I can handle this too. Or… maybe God thinks that I'm just a bad ass!

Now, I am not making light of the seriousness of what is to come. I know I will have ups and downs, but I have a great support system here and I have a positive attitude. I think that's a real good start for getting through this, right? I believe I am in good hands and in God's hands. What else does one need?

And so on to the business of getting appointments set up. Surgery is the next thing to come. I knew that was most likely going to happen when I felt the size of this thing manifesting inside of me. It's the options after surgery that's not quite clear to me yet, so I have some research to do. I don't like the idea of radiation or chemotherapy. I'm sure no Calypso patient does really. I plan to see my Acupuncturist and see what he might have to say about all of this. There has to be a more natural way of dealing with the aftermath than to pump chemicals into one's body. Again, I am optimistic about the options.

Social media….
I asked my family at first not to post anything on social media. It seems everyone lives their life out there for all to read and I didn't want that… at first. After speaking with Kelly, I told her maybe that was best to just get it out there and talk about it and keep people updated that way. In some ways this is a very personal matter, but I feel like maybe I can be an example to others of how to stay positive.

I can boo-hoo about this and have myself a nice little pity-party, sure. Or, I can accept it for what it is… a bit of Calypso. It's not the death sentence that everyone thinks it is. I know I am going to breeze through this. Okay, maybe I won't "breeze" but I certainly will get through it. I am a strong, independent woman and I have dealt with a lot over the years. There are worse things that could happen.

So I went with the Caring Bridge as a way to journal and share my thoughts and feelings about this new episode in my life.

November 7: Introspect….
I feel a little like George Bailey in "It's a Wonderful Life" right now. In the opening scene you see the clouds and heavens above and all these voices sending up prayers for poor old George. In just 24 hours, the very few people that I have shared the Calypso news with have sent out prayer chains to thousands. It's very touching to know that so many people can jump into action so quickly when called upon. I am so blessed to have such good friends and family.

The BED Team

Immediately I have my sister and two friends who swing into action. Bobbie, Eva and Dawn – the B.E.D. team. I know between these three amazing women, I will ease through this. I don't even have to ask – I know they will see me through it and that gives me great comfort. It's amazing that when given a piece of bad news, one can feel so immeasurably blessed!

On to the Oncology Surgeon…
The long process of calling for appointments and checking in to FMLA begins. This is where an assistant would come in handy! I was able to get an appointment to see the Oncology Surgeon today.

A mere two hours later…

The appointment at the Oncology Surgeon went really well, or at least as best I could expect under the circumstances. It was a lot of information thrown at me all at once. It's worse than I thought… probably because I thought I'd get off easy. A small tumor – cut it out, zap it and I'm back to my normal life. Okay, it's a bit more complicated than that.

In a nutshell, I am most likely looking at a double mastectomy. That was a hard pill to swallow. On the up-side, maybe I could end up with "the breasts of a 20 year old!"

Bobbie started a message board on Trello so we can share information with family members and close friends. She is so amazing and organized. I know I can never repay her kindness and I know she would never expect any repayment. That's not why she does what she does. I don't think she even realizes how amazing she is…but I think those close to her do!

I also have a BNN - Breast Nurse Navigator. I met with her right after seeing the doctor and she said her role is to answer my questions, make appointments and see that my "team" (doctors, nurses, etc) have all the information they need. She also gave me what I call the BBB - Big Breast Book. Before you guys get all excited, it's NOT a book about big breasts! It's a big BOOK about breast cancer. (Gee, I bet the guys were ready to order that up online)!

November 11:

All I can do now is patiently wait for test results to come back and more appointments to be set up. I am usually pretty prompt in taking care of anything, so this part is hard for me. Still, it's out of my hands and my need to control situations is going to be tested to the limits in the coming weeks, so might as well sit back and carry on "normal" as I can.

I am slowly telling people about the Calypso but mostly those not here in the Springs. I want to wait until I have a surgery date set. I just hope the Outdoor Group that I organize doesn't suffer much with my absence. I have a lot of good people that will hopefully band together and keep things going.

New boobs!

November 12, 2013

November 12... or some might count it as 11-12-13.

I saw the Plastic Surgeon today with my BED Team. It went very well and I like the doc and staff. He spent a good deal of time with us and explained the options very thoroughly. This type of surgery has come a long way. The BBB (Big Breast Book) is a bit outdated as to how the procedure is done and what it looks like. He showed us photos of patients with the similar disease and the before/after photos look identical. That's very promising!
So, there was a lot of boob-talk today. Bobbie and I joked that if we were guys we would have brought beer and cameras to the appointment! Oh, and the Doctor told me I had nice breasts – I guess that's quite a compliment coming from a plastic surgeon!

I am feeling a bit overwhelmed again with so much information. Bobbie and Eva both took notes. I am lucky to have extra ears to hear and document for me. Sure makes it easy for me. Next up is the appointment with the Medical Oncologist and they will decide if I need further tests to determine if the Calypso has spread to any other areas or organs. We should also have the genetic test back by then so we will be armed to the boobs with information and can hopefully get a surgery date on the calendar.

I almost sound anxious for this, don't I? Well, the sooner we get it done, the sooner I can get back to my regular scheduled programs! In the meantime, the waiting makes me feel like my life is more normal. I am hiking and walking every day trying to keep up my strength. I figure the stronger I am before surgery, the more quickly I will heal.

It occurred to me the other day while I was walking... it's reported that one in 8 women will get breast cancer. Instead of asking "why me" which I never did actually - I tell myself "God doesn't give us more than we can handle, so obviously the other 7 women were not as strong as I am. He knew I could deal with this and be an advocate and hopefully an inspiration to others facing the same problem." That also gave me great comfort, knowing that since I have this disease someone else will be healthy.

Feeling positive about the future - keeping faith in my support team, my physicians, nurses and all involved in this journey. Very blessed indeed!

 # Patiently waiting

November 13, 2013

I think "patiently waiting" is an oxymoron. Nobody likes to wait and not too many of us have the patience to wait. Still, what choice do I have? Carry on as normal...

I had a nice long hike at Palmer Park today. I am feeling really good too. It was a gorgeous day in the mid-60's. I am so glad I live in Colorado where the sun shines more than 300 days in the year. People wonder how I can have such a great attitude in dealing with this. Besides the wonderful friends and support that I have, a part of it is because I live here in God's country.

I saw my Acupuncturist. We just had a quick consult as to how he might help me. He said he could start treatment now to help boost my immune system and then help with side effects during treatment if needed. I'm going to just play it by ear right now. I already have lots of appointments and tests being done and he wants me in there three times a week.

I spent the evening tonight with some fun ladies over at Bobbie's house. It was great and we ate way too much but that's okay - it's all good. Laughter - the best medicine.

My next appointment is next Tuesday with the Medical Oncologist, whose name is really hard to pronounce. I hope to have the lab results back by next week as well so we should have a plan of action in place soon to kick some Calypso butt. Glad I have friends to go into battle with me and I will continue to journal and write my thoughts down here.

Thank you all for your love and support!

Healthy mind, healthy body, healthy soul

November 14, 2013

One piece of advice that I got from someone who has gone through this - walk every day no matter how you feel. I do this anyway and you all know how much I hike. Still, it will be crucial in my recovery to remember this.

I was on my walk today at lunch and just feeling "normal." Now my family would say that I've never been normal in my life, so how is it that Calypso can change that? So I guess I should amend that to be "My Version of Normal."

Anyway, walking and feeling MVoN and listening to some tunes on the ipod... it's in the 60's the sun is shining and it's a gorgeous day here in Colorado. I love this song that comes on by Kris Allen called "Live like we're dying." It talks about not passing up the opportunity to say "I love you" to those who have meaning in your life. "We've only got 86,400 seconds in a day to turn it all around or throw it all away." I think I have always lived my life this way and expressed my love and gratitude to my friends and family. I pray that it doesn't take a medical wake up call for people to live like they're dying.

I can't help but think that the volunteer work that I've signed up for doing hospice work is somehow connected to my Calypso situation. Seems strange to me that right about the time I signed up to volunteer, I find a lump in my breast. It will be interesting to see how these two life events are related. I do believe things like this and people we meet can be and are interconnected. I don't think we are all here on earth just to randomly walk around until we bump into people we like or love. It all happens for a reason.

So, yes on my walks I have a lot of time to think and sometimes it's profound, other times it's just random thought bouncing around as I stroll along. I'll let the readers decide which it was today.

I have been slowly getting the news out to more people. It's not an easy thing to share but the more people that know, the more prayers and positive thoughts will be out there and that all works in my favor. I know I am feeling very upbeat and positive... but then, I haven't seen or heard of any test results yet so I guess the old "Ignorance is bliss" statement could still apply here!

Nah, I do feel good and I know in my heart this is just a speed bump in my life's journey. It doesn't even matter what the test results show. I feel good about my decisions and the care I am receiving and especially my BED team and all the friends that have reached out to me to show their love and support. I just couldn't ask for more and I thank you all - Love and Gratitude!

 # Cosmic Connections

November 17, 2013

Another weekend has gone by and just waiting for Tuesday to get here. I don't know if we'll get all the results back by then, but I am hoping to have enough information to start to move forward. In ways, the waiting has been good. I've been hiking and spending time with friends as if nothing has changed.

I have been participating in a Webinar type series called "21 Days of Gratitude." It has really helped me keep perspective of what's important in life. Today was about the cosmic connections in our lives, which really hit home with me. I've always believed that we are all interconnected and that things do happen for a reason. I don't think I can say the word "grateful" comes to mind when I describe how I feel about having Calypso. But I am glad it was me who got it instead of someone who may not have been able to deal with it. Perhaps God knew I was strong enough to handle it and that I had a good support system, insurance, job assurance, etc. I will never know why I was chosen but I do know I don't question it either. I will accept it for what it is.

Whatever the outcome, I have no regrets. That's not to say that if, given the chance, I wouldn't go back and do things differently with my life, but I am not regretful. All the events of my life have lead me to be the person I am today. I am in the exact right place at the exact right time.

And so on this day, I am feeling unbelievably blessed. My friends have been rallying around me to show support and comfort. I have a great attitude and positive outlook, as do those around me.

I also wanted to post the topic of today's Gratitude session. Perhaps it will strike something in others as well. I am grateful for every cosmic connection in my life.

Often we meet someone and we feel like we've known them forever. Was it a previous life? Is it fate, karma, destiny?

Quantum Physics tells us that everything in the universe is energy and as such everything moves and vibrates at one speed or another. We live and move in a sea of energy. Is that person that we feel such a deep connection to vibrating at the same rhythm as we are? If so, we are entrained with them.

When you experience such a connection, your heart swells with overwhelming gratitude. We need those sweet moments, those heart openers. When our vibrations coincide with those of another person, we are entrained to be with them. We feel an indescribable closeness, and that affinity which leads us to perform life long bonds.

In a precisely ordered universe, the people we meet and the circumstances we encounter all encourage us to stretch and grow in consciousnesses. Be grateful for your interconnectedness. Give thanks for your teachers, your lovers, your confidants, your friends, and your family. Because they all appear to make our world a better place

# Don't let it get the breast of you

November 18, 2013

So, I was in a store today perusing the books and I see one that says "In the Garden of the Breast." Except it doesn't say breast, it says beast. Could it be that men had it right all along? It really is all about the boobs?

This isn't the first time this has happened either. I see the word breast everywhere now, even when it's not there. I think I need to get this surgery scheduled soon or I may end up the biggest boob of all!

I took the week off for vacation time that I will lose if I don't use it. I have medical leave for surgery and recovery still. I thought about taking a quick get-away but then a funny thing happened... my week got filled up. Guess I'll save that trip to Hawaii for later - like when I have my new perky boobs and I can go topless on Waikiki. (oops, my mother is going to read this).

It was a pretty nice day here in Colorado. I went to the dentist office only to discover that my appointment is December 18, not November 18. I've never been a month early for an appointment before. All was not lost - I still got to have lunch with my sister at one of our favorite spots - Schnitzelfritz. They make the best Reuben sandwich in town. Afterwards

I took a hike at Palmer Park and boy did that feel good to get out on a trail. There is no place else I'd rather be. I have a yoga class tonight and tomorrow we finally have the appointment with the medical Oncologist.

That's all the news for now... just wanted to keep you all "abreast" of the situation. Getting anxious, yes but I try not to let it get the breast of me!

 # Nature's Way

November 19, 2013

Well today was quite eventful.

It started with a visit to the Acupuncturist, which went very well. He told me a great story about a big news event in China. Seems this woman in her late 30's was diagnosed with some type of stage 3 terminal cancer. The doctors told her if there is anything she wants to do with her life to do it. She sells her house and everything she owns, takes the money and travels all around the world for 8 months. When she returns to China, she sees the doctor and they can find no cancer present.

Makes me think... hmmmm. I have a couple airline tickets to get me started - maybe at least to the east coast.... Nah, I could never pull that off! But I sure have been thinking about it all day!

So, the visit to the Oncologist went well except of course that she recommended chemotherapy, radiation and hormone treatment. To which I replied No, No, and uh... No. What else ya got doc?

None of these options really sound good. Chemo kills Calypso cells, yes but it also kills healthy cells. I understand that Calypso is a really powerful disease so it takes an equally powerful treatment plan but still - I'd like to keep my healthy cells just the same, thank you.

Radiation, well - do I really need to say why this sounds bad to me?

Hormone therapy - I passed on it the first time and it still doesn't look all that appetizing on the second course. She did mention that there is a study that I may qualify for that doesn't involve radiation but does require chemo. I'll sleep on that option.

So, what's left? Well, I may be able to go with my acupuncturist for the follow up treatment. It's a big decision and I've seen him work some pretty amazing medical miracles. I've talked to a lot of his patients while I am in the waiting room. See, it pays to be friendly to people.

I have a little time to ponder the choices. The main thing to do first is get rid of the ta-ta's and the creepy little friends that they've invited into my body. The Oncology Surgeon called me this afternoon and said we'll have a surgery date set by tomorrow and it will be in the next week or two. Oh crap - did I really tell her to schedule it asap?

They drew more blood and did an EKG today. I have a CT Scan on Thursday and a MRI on Friday. The CT Scan is just to rule out any other issues in the chest/abdomen area. The MRI is just to prove to my sister that my brain really IS normal! Well, I think the doctor may want to rule out any problems due to my recent headaches as well. But still, I will have test results that say I am normal in the head - so naner-naner-boo-boo to my sister!

So, things are moving along now. I just need to start thinking of my treatment options. The medical marijuana option is still out there, so like fer sure man, I'll totally think about killing some brain cells too.

We'll see how these next two tests go... not looking forward to the CT Scan with contrast. I have an "apple flavored cocktail" to drink before hand. I was given a disapproving look when I asked if I could add vodka to it. Friday's test only requires a Xanax on my part so who knows what I might write here afterwards.

I am happy to see so many visits to my journal. I hope it helps someone out there who might be dealing with the same situation. Things could always be a lot worse, so just count your blessings first!

 # T-minus 13

November 20, 2013

Well, the date is set for Tuesday, December 3rd at noon. Wonder if that's "high" noon? I know I will be high (sedated, high - same difference)!

After the long day yesterday of talking chemo, radiation, hormone therapy, blood work, EKG today seemed like a walk in the park. It actually was a walk in the park sort of... I had my acupuncture appointment and walked myself over there and back. It was very relaxing (as much as having needles stuck in you can be relaxing that is).

I'm glad things are coming together and I know this is just the beginning. It's a long road ahead, but with my support team and extended support team I feel so secure and comforted.

I am reading a book that I just happened upon the other day. It's a collection of short stories by a survivor and those around her who went through her ordeal of Calypso with her. It has some very thought provoking quotes all the way through the book, so I thought I would share some here.

"We have no right to ask when sorrow comes "Why did this happen to me?" unless we ask the same question for every moment happiness comes."

"God made the world round so we would never see too far down the road." - Isak Dinesen

"Worry is like a rocking chair. It gives you something to do, but it doesn't get you anywhere." - Winston Churchill

"If not for darkness, you wouldn't see the stars" - Ralph Waldo Emerson

"When the Japanese mend broken objects, they aggrandize the damage by filling the cracks with gold. They believe that when something's suffered damage and has a history, it becomes more beautiful."

I really like that last one.... but it does make me wonder if I might get some additional kind of "bling" for my new ta-ta's?

Just wanted to close this with something fun. It's the breast I can do you know.

Nothing left to say but "Ta-ta" for now!

 # Barium Cocktail anyone?

November 21, 2013

Today was a busy day... again. I wouldn't be this tired if I had worked all week!

So I woke up to snow, which made me smile. Then I remembered I have to go out today - smile turned upside down. Then I remembered I have my car in a garage now... okay, something resembling a smile returned.

I went to the hospice office for a couple hours to help with some admin work. I finished my hospice training a week ago but since I'll be out of it for a while, they really can't assign a patient to me to visit yet. At least I can contribute in other ways though. What a wonderful group of people. I still can't help but think that my signing up for hospice work right about the time I was diagnosed with Calypso isn't somehow related. Weird.

So I did a pre-op visit via the phone when I got home, then shortly after had my first barium cocktail. It definitely would have been better with vodka. Still - it was kind of like a lumpy, watered down milk with a bit of apple taste. Not as bad as some people have described but not something I will be stocking up on in the fridge either.

I met Dawn at the Med Center and got the CT Scan done. The tech asked me if I had one before and I told him yes, a very long time ago. It was when I had kidney stones and was very sick, so the IV contrast made me throw up. He was not too pleased to hear this. I assured him it was the kidney stones but he still didn't look too happy with me.

Anyway, that was uneventful - no vomiting much to his relief as he pushed me out the door.

I came home and made several loaves of pumpkin bread. This is quite an accomplishment because it started with two small pumpkins that I cut up, baked, pureed and then made the cake. That is as "from scratch" as it gets folks! Lick the spoon and call me Betty!!! (Crocker of course)

So, tomorrow is the brain MRI. I am guessing the results will look something like this... ??????? crap ???????? WTF ?????? UGH ?????

After that, I think I am tested out until surgery. Hopefully I didn't flunk any of these tests. If I did, will they punish me by putting a little bell or squeaky toy in my breast so it makes a weird noise when I move? Wouldn't that be a good (surgeon) joke!

Okay - enough of my weird thoughts for the day. It's kind of strange writing this down because I know people are going to read it. It's kind of like when you were little and someone took a peek at your diary. Better mind my P's and Q's! Of course "keeping a journal" sounds so much more grown up that "keeping a diary."

Until next time...

The good news and the bad...

November 22, 2013

Today was another busy day. I didn't realize that Calypso was such a time consuming event. Or just the previews leading up to the main event.

Dropping off forms, picking up instructions and prescriptions for after surgery. Love that idea though to have the pain pills before surgery. A quick visit to the acupuncture office, grocery store and back home. Since I had the MRI scheduled I took a Xanax to relax me. I've heard they are quite noisy. Good thing I put dinner in the crock pot prior to taking it though. Who knows what would have ended up in there!

My wonderful sister Eva drove me to this appointment, which was another uneventful outing. I pretty much napped through that test (much like I did in high school). I even got a call on the results later that day to say all was normal. Yes, my brain is normal... who knew?

So, everything is looking good for surgery. Now we just wait.... oh, and give thanks in there too. Looking forward to seeing my mom and sister for Thanksgiving!

The bad news does not pertain to me. Sorry if the title was a little worrisome. I learned today that my very dear friend Jim has pancreatic cancer. I am still in disbelief and a little heart broken. Is this some warped Chinese calendar year called "year of the cancer?" I think I am more upset about this than my own diagnosis. I have yet to get all the details but I am praying already for a good outcome for my dear friend.

And so I ask those of you who are praying for me, please also add a prayer for my friend, who means a great deal to me. We all know how powerful prayer can be, so let's get the prayer chain started.

 # Prayer request

November 23, 2013

Just a quick note for today, and a bit more somber than my previous posts. My dear friend Jim was just diagnosed with advanced stage pancreatic cancer and now my heart is breaking. We've been having some very long and candid conversations about it and the eventual end of life.

I had signed up to volunteer for hospice work and just completed the required 15 hours of training. I would have never dreamed that my first patient would be a close friend. If I thought being diagnosed with breast cancer wasn't the greatest news, I can't imagine being given a time line on my life. He says our circumstances are inter-connected and I agree, though how exactly remains to be seen.

I have been praying non-stop for him and I hope some of you will too. He now needs them more than I do.

Thank you all - love and hugs.

T-minus 7

November 26, 2013

Well, by this time next week I will be getting ready to go to the hospital for surgery. I think we have all our T's crossed and those I's are dotted, so nothing more to do but wait.... oh, and eat turkey!

It's going to be a busy week/weekend. I have about 30 friends going to a happy hour tonight that will benefit the Trails & Open Space Coalition. Tomorrow I am going on a nice long hike with friends... still working on building up my strength before surgery!

My mom and sister from Omaha are coming in on Thanksgiving. I'll be making rounds to visit friends that day as well. Friday evening I am spending with some friends who are having a party on my behalf. It's very touching to have such caring friends here.

Saturday evening we are doing a "stroll" downtown, then a wine/painting party at the Sweet Elephant. I've always wanted to do one of those. It's where you go and paint on a canvas (with instruction obviously) and drink wine as you paint. I'm thinking with enough wine, I could be the next Picasso!

Sunday is the day Kelly gets here. I am very anxious to see her. She will be my primary care taker for the first 5 days after surgery, which just brings me such comfort. After 32 years, we've been through everything together including previous surgeries (mine and hers). This also allows us a day or two of fun before she has to earn her keep!

Sometime over the weekend I am going to put up Christmas decorations. I have a 7 foot tree and lots of decor, so I am ready to deck the halls! I haven't done that in years so I'm looking forward to having a tree and hopefully as Christmas gets closer I can have a holiday party here.

I am still spending a lot of time with my terminally ill friend and continue to pray for a miracle... whatever God's will be. This time of year is very emotional for me... always has been.

I love Christmas and the holiday season, but I find myself crying at Hallmark commercials for Pete's sake! I'm very touched by all the visitors to my blog and of course love the comments and hearts. I will continue to post as this journey continues. I am so very blessed and feeling much love and support.

Until next time... "ta-ta" again!

Giving thanks

On this Thanksgiving Day, I am reflecting on the events of the past few weeks and feeling absolutely overwhelmed with gratitude. Not that I wish anyone to have to deal with Calypso in his or her life. I do however, wish for everyone to have the opportunity at some point in their lives to stop and realize how blessed they really are. No matter how much or how little we have in life, there is always someone who has it worse.

Every person you encounter is there for a reason, a season, a moment or a lifetime. You never know the journey they have been on or are currently on. Don't make assumptions or judge too quickly, but reach out and get to know them. That person could change your life in ways you never dreamed possible.

I have been so fortunate to have this life event come along. Again, feeling a bit like George Bailey in "It's a Wonderful Life." When you stop for a moment and look around and the lives that you've touched and the people who have come in and out of your life, it's almost impossible to say anything but "wow." Or as my mom might say "Holy Crap!"

I have always been a believer of living a simple life. I don't have a lot and don't need a lot... of **things** that is. Now friendships on the other hand... I can never have enough of those.

So, today I have much to be thankful for... a roof over my head, food in the house and a means to support myself; my health, my friends and my family. The list could go on and on. From the comfort of sleeping in a warm bed on a cold night to waking up and looking at those gorgeous mountains to the west... it truly is a wonderful life. Enjoy each new day and live it as if it was your last.

Happy Thanksgiving to all - count your blessings!

Party time!

November 30, 2013

As if the past few weeks haven't been enough to show me how many friends I have that care.... Laura and Craig threw a party for me last night that was absolutely amazing. So many of my friends were there and most of the ladies wore pink shirts to support the ta-ta's.... literally.

Lots of food and fun and more boob talk. I guess this is one of those times when it's okay for boob talk... for both men and women. My favorite line of the evening came from Anne (as we were talking boobs) when she said "I am having a hard time resisting feeling my own boobs right now." I thought I was going to wet myself I laughed so hard.

Second to that was Dawn telling about when she lived in California and how she can spot a boob job immediately (as she points)... "real, fake, fake, real, fake etc."

Talking, laughing and telling stories with my friends has got to be one of the best ways I can think of to spend my time prior to surgery. Laughter really is the best medicine. Too bad we can't bottle it up in mega doses. I'm sure it would be the cure for Calypso and many other diseases.

My BFF Kelly is coming in a day early, so I am waiting for a call to meet her and pick her up today. Then we are going to Old Colorado City for dinner, a stroll then the wine & painting class. I am really enjoying this time off work... now how do I make this last and still manage to pay my bills? I'll have to ponder that one.

I am getting ready to deck the halls today. I pulled Christmas crap (oops I mean decor) from the garage so I have to go through it and see what is in there. My problem is I go to after-Christmas sales and buy even more CC (Christmas Crap) and box it away. Then when I pull it out the following year, it really is like Christmas since I don't remember what I bought!

This will be the first time in years that I have put up a tree, so I am looking forward to having people over during the holidays. Just more incentive to speed up my recovery so I can enjoy more time with friends.

I think I must have been a very good girl this year because Santa already brought me my presents... good friends, family, laughter and love. All I can say is "wow."

Thank you all for the great time last night... hope to see you all again very soon! Ta-Ta for now!

# The adventure begins...

December 2, 2013

It's late Monday night... I have about an hour left to eat something if I choose... maybe one last handful of M&Ms? Not really hungry though - just a little anxious and nervous. Still thinking good thoughts though. Kelly has been such a good person to have around these past couple days. She's strong and positive minded, just like me. She somehow instinctively knows what I need to hear and all the right things to do. God bless her.

So, we decided to watch a Christmas movie tonight and very appropriately selected "It's a Wonderful Life." Of course this movie makes me bawl like a baby. From the time old George is on the bridge and exclaims "Zuzu's petals" until the end when she says "Teacher says every time a bell rings, an angel gets his wings" I am boo- hooing and laughing at the same time. Watching George run through the town screaming "YEAH" just gets me. It's my favorite movie ever.

So after posting a small blurb online and seeing so many replies, I am still feeling like George at that final moment when you realize what a wonderful life it really is. I couldn't have imagined that this whole ordeal would bring out the love and friendships that it has. Unfortunate that it has to be something like Calypso that brings people together, but really I know now that it could be even a small favor to ask and I have plenty of friends who would jump into action.

Thank you - those two little words seem insignificant to show my appreciation for the friends who have been helping me, supporting me and comforting me over the past few weeks. I wish I could find the words to express my gratitude properly but I am at a loss. Feeling very blessed and loved. I hope that is enough for those who have helped... knowing they each contributed to this feeling.

I don't wish Calypso or any other unfortunate disease or illness upon anyone... however, if there is ever a need for one of my friends, I would jump at the opportunity to give back at least as much, if not more comfort and support as I have been given.

So, tomorrow we say ta-ta to the ta-ta's. Not to worry - the boob jokes will live on in future blogs. Just because the boobs are gone doesn't mean the jokes are! The breast is yet to come you know!

Guess it's time to try and get some sleep. Not too worried if it doesn't come easy because I will catch up on it the rest of the week.

Surgery update will be online tomorrow. And I will hopefully be coherent enough to blog by the end of the week. If I write anything about dancing bears in my hospital room, you will all understand that is the morphine talking.

A final ta-ta and thank you all from the bottom of my heart for your love and support!

Ready for surgery, sporting my new PJ's and hair style.

# What doesn't kill you makes you stronger

December 4, 2013

I am home from the hospital and just in time. With the temps dropping and snow falling I can't think of a better place to be than snuggled up in my bed.

Surgery went about as well as I could have expected. My BED team gave me such great support along with all the well wishes from friends and family near and afar. The medical team went above and beyond. It truly was the best care one could ever hope for.

I believe in the power of prayer and affirmations. I gave a copy of my affirmations to my BED team and to the Anesthesiologist to read to me prior to surgery. Made all the difference in the world. And as they wheeled me off, I told my team "See you in a few hours... or for me a few minutes!"

I had a private room with a private nurse (two actually) and Kelly stayed with me and slept in a recliner. Cuz that's just what a BFF of 32 years does! Of course she snored all night too, but I had such a nice mix of meds that it didn't really faze me.

So, what's next? I have four drains in me - two of them will come out next week and the other two will come out the following week. The pathology on the tumor will be back probably next week, then we can start to talk about treatment. I hope to get in to a clinical study and maybe not have to do chemo, radiation and/or hormone therapy. At least there are options and the treatments have come a long way. Images of nausea and vomiting during chemo are no longer the norm. I am going to wait until after the New Year to start anyway and just enjoy the holidays with family and friends. Tis the season you know!

I am in good spirits and feeling great. I couldn't ask for more love and support from friends and family. I know I repeat myself over and over but I feel truly blessed. It's a very comforting feeling to know what's important in life and it has nothing to do with possessions, money, power, status, career, etc. I have a network of friends who care and that means more to me than anything.

So, I hope you will continue this ride with me on the road to recovery. We made it over the speed bump and may have a few detours or road blocks ahead, but I know at the end of the road, there is a trail head just waiting for me to get back on it!

Until then... happy trails to all!

Post-op update

Dec 7, 2013

Well, here it is just 4 days after surgery and I am off all pain meds and doing quite a bit for myself around the house. Kelly says her job is done. I still have restrictions on lifting things and raising my hands over my head so dancing and "raising the roof" are definite no-no's!

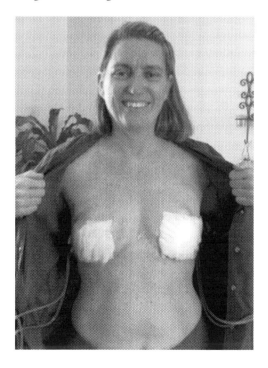

I have been showing off my new chest to anyone who asks. My friend Anne was the first to ask for a photo, so I bared (almost) all. I've lost all modesty during this process! I do think it's rather fascinating so I guess I just assume other people think so too! I have four drains in - two on each side. Two come out on Tuesday, which I guess makes it a sort of "Two-fer-Tuesday" now doesn't it? The other two come out about a week later. Once those are out I will feel a bit more normal. Again, that's MVON (My Version Of Normal)!

Technically I can drive since I am no longer on the pain meds, but I really have no need or desire just yet. I don't want to push things and end up back in bed. I really owe my speedy recovery to all those positive thoughts and prayers... tons of them from what I can calculate. I appreciate it so much. I know my own attitude and expectations of a quick and easy recovery had a bit to do with it too.

I did find out that the tumor was a bit larger than estimated at 4.8cm. There was also a second tumor at 0.8cm. They got clean margins on both, meaning they got it all out. They took a patch of lymph nodes - 22 total and found 6 of those with a bit of Calypso action as well. Unfortunately this means that I won't qualify for any clinical studies and will have to go with chemo and radiation.

Yeah, that bummed me out at first, but it is what it is. I can't change it and the alternative is to do nothing but that's a bit like rolling the dice on my life. Not the practical thing to do, right? And some of you know this has been the year of doing the practical thing for me. I'm actually getting rather good at it! Who knew I was capable of such rational though?

I have some follow up appointments this week and will see the Acupuncturist. Other than that, I think I need to find a hobby or boredom will set in rather quickly! I do have that stack of books to read.

I'm thoroughly enjoying all the yummy meals that friends are bringing and the visits. I just need to remember to limit them to about an hour. I had several today and was left feeling wiped out. It was my first full day off the pain meds so I was feeling pretty good though!

Thanks again all for taking this journey with me. Just like those hiking trails that I love... it's always more enjoyable when shared with friends.

# Tis the season

Dec 8, 2013

Wow - I just saw that I have over 600 visits on my blog thus far. That is truly amazing to me. I've always enjoyed writing and telling stories but never really felt like what I had to say would be anything people would actually want to read. I guess it took Calypso to give me my voice.

I've had a really great weekend. I stopped taking the pain meds (narcotics) on Friday so I've had a bit more lucidity, which allowed me to 1. Stay awake more during the day and 2. Enjoy many visitors! Both excellent for my recuperation and well-being. I can't say it enough that being surrounded by caring, loving people has been crucial in my quick recovery.

I had many visitors stop by both Saturday and Sunday, which just made my day. Bobbie and Terry came over tonight and cooked dinner for me, which was just wonderful.

It was so hard to say good-bye to Kelly and I just can't imagine having gone through this without her. After 32 years, she and I have been through just about everything together. Certainly many surgeries – both hers and mine! This one was probably the toughest but it only strengthened an already unbreakable friendship. My life would not be complete without her. I know she left here reassured that I have an amazing group of friends and the support that I need since she couldn't stay indefinitely!

So, what's next? Christmas of course!

The pathology report wasn't as good as I had hoped but I will do what I need to do to fight this battle and I have an army of supporters, so winning is the only option I can foresee.

That being said, my focus for the rest of the year is to spend time with friends and family and enjoy the holiday season. I hope to get out for some walks and hikes soon and build up my strength for this battle that we are about to undertake. I hope to maybe get some volunteer time in and give back to show my appreciation for all of those who gave so unselfishly to me.

Most of all, I want to focus on the Christmas holiday itself. I absolutely love this time of year. Maybe it's because people seem to be a bit kinder and more generous. My ultimate wish would be that we could all feel this way all year round. It may sound corny but it really is about peace on earth and goodwill towards men.

A friend told me today that he liked my perspective about the important aspects of a gift being the circumstances and thoughts that surround the giving of the gift, not the gift itself. I thought that was one of the kindest complements I have ever heard.

I know my posts have turned a bit sappy lately. That has nothing to do with the Calypso. I get this way around the holidays every year. It starts around Thanksgiving and ends shortly into the New Year. It truly is a joyous season... wish it could last a bit longer. Lord knows the merchandisers try to stretch it out by putting up Christmas displays in October. Such a shame that all the marketing is geared towards the commercial and materialistic perspective. So far from what the season is really about.

This is just my opinion, but if you really want to give the ultimate Christmas gift this year... consider spending quality time with someone.

Yes, it could be family or friends, but to take it a step further - visit a nursing home or hospital, volunteer a little of your time. That is a gift to both yourself and someone else. It may or may not be returned but hopefully will be "re-gifted!"

I hope to see many of my friends again soon. I miss the trails and I'll get back out there soon for some short hikes and socializing. Don't be shy about coming to visit either - I am enjoying the company!

And if I don't see you in the coming weeks, have a blessed holiday season and best wishes in the New Year!

A draining day

Dec 10, 2013

So, I had two of the four drains removed today - yeah! I'm anxious to get the other two out so I can sleep on my side again. Ah, it's the little comforts that make life enjoyable.

It was pretty weird watching the doc pull the tubes out. It didn't hurt, but it was much like a little worm sliding across my chest! I am left with some pretty wrinkly breasts but that's only because the fillers/temporary implants only have 300 cc's of fluid in them and they removed 500. When I go back next week, he will fill me up with another 50 cc's and continue to do so until I say "when." This is pretty fascinating stuff, right? I hope you are all enjoying this breast education as much as I am. I've always been fascinated with all things medical and the human body really is quite interesting.

After the doctor appointment, we went to lunch at Hacienda for some yummy Mexican cuisine, my favorite. Bobbie took me to Sprouts to get some fresh produce, and then I came home and took a nap. My first outing in a week and it wore me out! Makes me wonder how my outing tomorrow will go. I am doing a short hike at Palmer Park with a few friends. No climbing or rock hopping involved, so no worries. Just need to "get out and blow the stink off me" as my mother likes to say. She has some pretty good ones, doesn't she?

I had a few more visitors tonight - Pam and Anne. We always have such wonderful conversation and they are good friends. Makes me happy to just enjoy having people stop by and visit or call, leave messages online, etc. All of it keeps my spirits high and reminds me how very blessed I am to have so many people who continually show how much they care.

The rest of the week holds a few more follow up appointments and acupuncture visits, then hopefully getting outside to enjoy the weather this weekend now that the cold snap has lost it's snap!

The bunnies will be relocated back to "their room" tomorrow evening. I had moved them downstairs while Kelly was here to make room. They didn't seem to mind much. They are pretty flexible as long as the food comes on a regular basis.

And so, another "wrinkle" in time goes by... across my chest. They just look kind of sad for the moment. But I do believe I have a perky future to look forward to!

Keep calm and hike on!

Dec 11, 2013

The weather finally cooperated today so I did my first post-op hike just 8 days after surgery. Just did a short walk around the Mesa trail, which was about 2+ miles. I'm feeling good but I know better than to push it too much. Good company on a crisp, clear Colorado day... now this is the way to a speedy recovery!

The forecast looks better, so I hope to continue to get out and build up my strength. I'm going to need it for when the battle begins next month. Calypso doesn't stand a chance against my army and me!

I was given a card at the docs office yesterday to carry with me with the information on my temporary fillers. I found myself wondering if it's like a library card so people (guys) can "check me out." Keep in mind here I am not on drugs... this is just one of the many ways I amuse myself.

I have lunch being brought to me again today from Mateka. How nice is that? Having people bring me food and come and cook for me? I could get used to this!

Tonight, Eva, Paul and the girls are visiting to relocate the buns back upstairs. That will give me my dining room back so I can enjoy meals at the table again. Looking forward to having friends over during the holidays.

Seems a bit strange to not be working right now but I am certainly keeping busy with follow up appointments, visitors and just keeping current on what's going on out there in the world! I could never imagine myself not working and I have only ever been unemployed once for about three months. That was just enough for me to enjoy a bit, but not get too bored. Of course, living in Colorado I doubt I would ever get bored if I wasn't working!

And here are some special M&M's that Bobbie had made for me. I was so happy until she told me they were for sharing! I'm not really good at sharing my chocolate.

Reality check

Dec 12, 2013

Today was a reality check for me. Up until now I kept telling myself "it's just Calypso" - no big deal. I realize now that the surgery was probably the easiest part of this. And I am lucky because it truly was easy for me.

I had my follow up appointment with Dr. Pomerenke and we talked a lot about chemotherapy and radiation. We also talked to the breast nurse navigator for a while and asked lots of questions and got lots of information. Seems they are going to take a very aggressive approach to treating me.

I am scheduled to have the port-a-cath put in on January 7th and chemo will start shortly after that. I am meeting with the Oncology Nurse Practitioner next week so will probably get more info then as to what type of cocktail I will be getting. Pick your poison and it's all poison. It's hard for me to comprehend what the coming months will be like for me. I have worked so hard these past few months to get in good shape, eating better and losing weight. To think that the next few months will be out of my control is a hard pill to swallow.

Still, everything happens for a reason. I am convinced that I lived in the south for so many years to teach me patience... because they just do things in their own good time in the south.

I'm still unsure why I was chosen to have this disease but I still tend to think it's to be a positive role model on how to deal with unpleasant situations. I have heard so many stories over the past weeks from so many people who have been through much worse. It really puts things in to perspective for me. Many women have been through this and survived for many, many years to come so I know I can do it too. I just pray for the courage to face it head on with my army of supporters.

I am so very blessed to have so many friends who are there for me. After having a bit of a melt down this afternoon, Anne came over and spent some time with me. We had wine and chatted and I felt so much better. It's nice to know if I am having a rough day I can count on my friends to help me through it. I am thinking that a little wine (with the whine), good friends and chocolate can pretty much cure anything!

So, back to chemo... right now it looks like about 8 rounds, once a week every 2-3 weeks. Once that is done I will have about 5 weeks of radiation, which will be every day. That's a very quick process compared to chemo. It sounds like chemo is the really bad part. That will most likely take me into late spring, early summer before I am finished... and bald. I guess if you have to be bald, summer is a better time than winter. I just gotta remember to use extra sunscreen!

I was ready for a "new do" anyway... they say sometimes your hair comes back completely different, so I could end up with red curls or something weird like that! I wonder if I could get a wig like the Princess Leah buns from Star Wars in the meantime! Wouldn't that be a conversation starter!

That's the update for now... I also get a chemo class soon, so will share what I learn there. I wonder if I flunk the class if I can just skip it? Nah, didn't think so....

Long day and I even got Buzz (my car) out and drove to the store and back. Gotta blow the stink off of me AND the car these days!

More adventures tomorrow and over the weekend, so time for some shut-eye.

Better days ahead... like fall/winter 2014???

Upa-downa

Dec 15, 2013

The longer I am on this journey, the more I realize it isn't like a ride in the car, bus, train, etc. It is more of a roller coaster. There are struggles to chug-chug-chug to the top and when you finally get there, you have a brief moment of "ahhhh" right before the plunge of thrill and terror back down.

Overall, this was a good weekend. I spent a good deal of time cooking on Saturday, which I have been enjoying more and more lately. I haven't done a lot of this until I moved into the duplex. When I moved to Colorado, I lived with Eva and Paul and let's face it, when you have a sister that puts on a mighty fine dinner every night, there just isn't a reason that compels me to cook. Fortunately, the duplex I am in now is good space for entertaining and I am enjoying cooking, baking and having friends over.

Sunday I got to go hiking again with Julie. She just moved to Dallas in October and I miss her so much. I'm glad we got to catch up and will do more catching up when she comes back next week. She always puts a smile on my face.

After taking a nap (all that fresh air, right?) I went to the Fine Arts Center with some friends to see a one-woman play called "The 12 dates of Christmas." It was really good... I'm always so impressed with these actors that can carry off a show single handedly and hold the audiences interest. Makes me miss the theatre in Montgomery... I loved working there!

After spending some time with Eva, Paul and the girls this evening for dinner I am back home and ready for some shut-eye.

I am doing another hike tomorrow and then more doctors follow up appointments on Tuesday. The first appointment was with the plastic surgeon, then the oncologist. There is the roller coaster ride again. I get the last two drains out and filled up a bit more. Glad to have those drains out so I can sleep on my side again. It's those little things in life that make me so happy. Filling up more I have mixed feelings on. The temporary implants are not comfortable but I hope it's just a temporary thing. I think I am getting the feeling back but I'm not sure the timing is great since he will be injecting saline in those things!

Oncology just scares the crap out of me to be perfectly honest. The more I learn about chemo, the less interested I am in it. They have recommended a trio called TAC. I won't bother with the drug names or pseudo names, aka's and such. Suffice it to say, none of those names have less than 4 syllables! There are some pretty scary side effects and toxicity to each, so I would like to discuss alternatives. Not sure why they want to treat me so aggressively... what did I ever do to them?

So looks like this week will be more of the ride... up a bit, down a bit - aka... upa-downa.

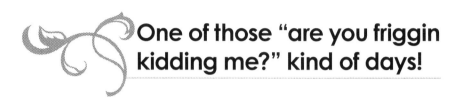One of those "are you friggin kidding me?" kind of days!

Dec 17, 2013

The roller coaster ride continues....

I had a pretty good weekend - visiting with friends, getting out for some short walks/hikes and enjoying the nice weather. Monday I went hiking with Jim and Tomah (the dog) and did a good bit at Palmer Park. I love that park - mainly because it's just a few blocks from my house but also because it has numerous trails so I can change the scenery a bit whenever I feel like it.

I had lunch with Ivy after my hike on Monday - tried Smash Burger for the first time. My official opinion is YUM! I enjoyed some good, uplifting conversation and catching up. I didn't even have to take a nap in the afternoon, so I slept a little better that night.

Tuesday was filed with more of the roller coaster ride. I saw the plastic surgeon first thing for what I thought was going to free me of these drains. Not so fast... still putting out too much fluid, so they can't come out. Well crap. I told him I was ready to pull them out myself and he cautioned me not to do so else I would get fluid build up and create more problems. Okay, so I was just joking anyway.

He also filled me up with another 100cm of saline. Now these boulders that I carry on my chest are rock-like and feel enormous. They aren't of course, but the pressure is rather uncomfortable. That elephant is back sitting on my chest. The fillers sit under the muscle and that muscle has to be stretched to accommodate the permanent implant. Still - I think it's time I said WHEN - I am full already.

So, visit number one did not go quite as planned. I came home for a bit then we had an appointment with the Nurse Practitioner at the Oncology office. Except when we got there she said the Doctor wanted to speak with me personally instead, so we had to reschedule for next week. On Christmas Eve to be precise. I have voiced my concerns over the chemo cocktail they want to prepare for me... "Thank you very much, it sounds delicious, but I am trying to cut back on chemicals. Call it a New Years Resolution."

I just need to hear more options. After doing some research on the chemicals and reading alternatives offered I am hopeful that we can meet in the middle somewhere between "killing all the cells that make me Laura" and "winging it." This is all really scary crap, let me tell ya!

We then met with a social worker who is able to help me apply for financial assistance, get my affairs in order for living will and medical Power of Attorney, etc. They also offer counseling and support in many other ways. I like the team that I have at Memorial Hospital. They really have come together to offer a full package. Kind of like an all-inclusive vacation - which is what I could really use about now!

When I finally got home, I had to get a little frustration out so I boo-hoo'd for a while. It's just necessary sometimes. I think it was mostly because my boobs hurt. I was ready to call the doc and tell him to remove these things, but I'm glad I held off making that call. I took my half bath/shower and washed my own hair, which felt great. I rigged up a bungee cord on the shower curtain to hold my drains & tubes to allow me to wash my hair. I don't think there is much in the world that a bungee, duct tape or WD40 can't resolve.

I felt much better after cleaning up so I called Anna - another survivor who offered some insight and encouragement. This also made me feel better since her situation is/was similar to my own. She is a 16-year survivor so things have come a long way. She had the same cocktail they are proposing for me with minimal side effects, so I am a bit more hopeful.

I took a little time to organize my thoughts tonight (since my new 2014 planner refills arrived and I was feeling in an organizing mood). I came across my affirmations from surgery so I decided to revise them for chemo. I may record them or just recite them while getting treatments. If it works as well as it did for my surgery, this will be a breeze! Okay - that's super optimistic, so let's just say it should be quite helpful.

I have an appointment on Friday with the Radiologist - even though that won't start for a few months. Other than that and my appointment on Christmas Eve, I think I am done for the year, so I hope to relax and enjoy some holiday cheer with family and friends. Something nice to look forward to!

Let's party like it's 1999 ya'all!

 # Random thoughts

Dec 19, 2013

The past two days have been rather uneventful, but I still felt I should write a little something to appease my ever-growing audience. Just kidding... my celebrity isn't quite going to my head yet. Besides if I had to encounter Calypso to become famous I'd rather be an unknown.

The elephant sitting on my chest has been replaced with something more like a bear (appropriate for Colorado you know). There is still pressure there but it's not quite as uncomfortable. I am still getting acupuncture and he tells me to slow down a bit after treatments and not try climbing any mountains just yet. That was rather odd since I thought moving around more helped with recovery. I took his advice just the same for the past few days and other than some Christmas shopping, haven't been as active. You know Christmas shopping a week before can be quite the workout! I didn't have to throw any punches though.

I don't know if filling up my chest worked or the lessened activity but the drains are slowing down on fluid output so I am counting on getting them removed on Tuesday. Yep - I get to see two doctors on Christmas Eve! And you thought getting a lump of coal in your stocking was bad? I get to talk chemo and have drains pulled out of me... Oh, how very merry!

Bobbie is taking a week off for Christmas... I don't know if I can function without her! Actually, I am physically doing quite well but I will miss her.

She deserves time off anyway. That leaves me with my "ED" team for my appointments next week and we'll get the job done.

My spirits are high again... must be all the Christmas music I've been listening to. Holly Jolly Christmas, Winter Wonderlands, and Rocking around the Christmas Tree! I have also been watching some of those Christmas movies. Not as many as I had hoped, but some new ones from last year. I honestly don't know where the time goes. I am not working yet the days just fly by and I haven't really accomplished all that I wanted to do. I guess staying off the computer might help me to be more productive.

I hope everyone is looking forward to Christmas as much as I am. It's my favorite time of year. People are a little kinder (except on black Friday) and there is a festive atmosphere all around. Too bad we can't wrap that up and put it under the tree for folks to open and wear all year long!

Less than a week away... I ho-ho-hope you all have a blessed Christmas!

# Keeping abreast of things

Dec 22, 2013

I can't believe it's almost Christmas!

I have been enjoying the times spent with family and friends and the visitors who have come by. It's just so heart warming to know how many people out there take the time to call, email, text, or visit. I am so very blessed.

I'm still waiting to get the last two drains out from surgery. It will be three weeks on Tuesday - Christmas Eve. I hope to get them out then and I am putting out less fluid so it looks good right now. I do need to talk to the plastic surgeon a bit more though as the temporary implants or "fillers" are driving me nuts! It's like carrying around two boulders that continually push into my chest. It's surprising how much pressure it puts on my whole torso and I feel it in my upper back as well. If this is how it's going to be for the next few months, I am ready to have them removed and skip reconstruction. I don't know if there are other options but this is kinda miserable.

Okay, enough whining... I just thought getting perky new boobs was going to be a good thing! It's hard to know if this is normal or not.

I have been off work for over a month now and I can honestly say that I have never felt so UN-productive! I honestly don't know where the time goes. How is it when we are working full time, we can get more accomplished than when I am not working? I am pretty organized and good with time management but honestly I never know what day it is anymore! It's like that movie Groundhog Day - it just keeps repeating!

I have two appointments on Tuesday this week - the Oncologist to talk chemo and the Plastic Surgeon to talk drains and fillers. I don't know how you are spending your Christmas Eve but I'm sure it can't be this exciting! I am anxious to get more info on the chemo option. It's a bit scary but I've got lots of questions and will use my resources to educate myself before we make a final decision. Not to scare anyone, but opting for no chemo is a valid option. I know it's risky but it is something I am considering. I am also not real keen on the idea of radiation. I meet with the Radiologist on Friday so I'll get more info then and I have several months before that would start so I can gather more info in the meantime there as well.

These are big decisions and I am not taking them lightly. I just want to consider ALL options and not just take the "one stop shop" type approach. I have learned quickly that all Calypso cases are different and all people are different in how they react. It's going to take a lot of education on my part before I can decide what is best.

Fortunately for me, my BED team and friends and family all understand that it's my decision and will support me in whatever I decide. Again I am lucky to have so much support and I don't know how anyone could go through something like this alone. I pray that anyone who has to experience Calypso can get into a support group of some kind.

Looking forward to spending Christmas Eve with a few friends and Christmas Day with my sister, her hubby and kids. Especially looking forward to some turkey and dressing! YUM!

I hope you all enjoy time with family and friends and have a blessed holiday. Until next time... Merry Merry!

# All I want for Christmas is my drains pulled out!

Dec 24, 2013

I got a very nice gift from the plastic surgeon today... he removed those last two drains! I rewarded him with a bag of my special M&M's.

Today was a bit overwhelming but I think I am getting a little better each time at handling being overwhelmed. I had an appointment with the Oncologist this morning... my ED team (minus Bobbie).. I really like her. She is from Africa and very personable, easy to talk to and ask and answer questions with. We all like her actually... and her name is rather fun to say.

Anyway, we talked about options and recommendations. We also plugged in all the data on me to an adjuvant website that tells what the prognosis looks like depending on what treatment I choose. Without any treatment, the chances of recurrence are high. With full treatment it goes down significantly. That may seem like a no-brainer but it was good for me to see the graph and numbers.

So, what we are looking at is two different types of chemo, starting mid-January. One will be 4 rounds every two weeks, then the next will be weekly for 12 weeks. Once that is done, I will start radiation - probably every day for 3-6 weeks. I meet with the Radiologist on Friday so that is to be confirmed yet. I also get to take a hormone pill for the next 5 years.

Once all of this is done, then it's back to the plastic surgeon to swap out the fillers for the real deal. Possible problems there are that radiation could possibly damage the breast tissue, which would mean taking some muscle from the back and moving it to the breast. We'll cross that bridge when and if we come to it. Perhaps I can find a way to jump that darn bridge!

Like I said - overwhelmed with information today. It's good to get the big picture but lots of different things can come up during this trip so I am learning to just take it one step at a time. It's like climbing a 14er... slow and steady and just focus on each step. Eventually you reach the goal and hopefully when it's all over I will be feeling grateful to be alive!

I am so looking forward to spending some time with family and friends for now... oh and to take a full shower again! Better check the size of that water heater cuz it's gonna be a long one!

I am having a few friends over tonight for Christmas Eve dinner and to watch "A Christmas Story." Tomorrow I will be going over to Eva & Paul's house and have Christmas with them. I've enjoyed picking up little things for the girls to unwrap.

Jim is going along to have Christmas with us. I am so glad he will be joining us, as we both know this will be his last one and I'd like to make it a special day for him. I feel honored that he wants to spend it with my family.

I have so much to be grateful for. It's going to be a long journey in 2014 but I am assuredly not going to travel it alone. I am blessed beyond belief with friends who are wiling to walk along with me, hold my hand or give me a hug when I need it and help me to smile when I want to cry.

One of my favorite sayings "That which doesn't kill you only makes you stronger." It's going to be put to the test very soon!

I wish all of my friends and family a very blessed holiday season. Be grateful for all that you have... and I am not talking about possessions or material things. The really important things in life cannot be seen or touched - they are heart felt.

God bless, Merry Christmas, Happy New Year and most of all THANK YOU from the bottom of my heart!

# Talkin' bout my radiation!

Dec 27, 2013

Today's appointment was all about the radiation. I was a bit hesitant about this... just seems so scary thinking of getting zapped every day for several weeks. They assured me I would not be radioactive afterwards. I would assume that somebody at some point asked that question. It might be a good parlor trick if that were true, right?

I do like the Radiologist... she was very smiley. I'm not sure how a doctor who deals with patients needing radiation would be so smiley while giving them this kind of information. She must really like what she does. It must work too because I liked her and decided that yes, I would be getting the radiation after chemo. That won't happen until around late July, early August by my estimates. They will start a few weeks after chemo is done. So that will put my new boobs in place probably somewhere in late September, early October. Guess they might be a birthday present for me! This is all kinda filling up my year... 2014 is going to be quite the adventure!

I've been very lucky really in that I have liked all my doctors... and I am getting quite a collection of business cards of doctors lately! For someone who never used a sick day (except for appointments) in the 13 years I've been with American Express and only had a Family Practitioner for a once a year visit, I now have an army of docs!

I have been getting out and walking or hiking again every day. Building up my strength before the adventure begins. I am still processing the information given and looking online and getting advice from other survivors. Every person is different and reacts differently so I guess it's just again, a matter of keeping a positive mindset and trusting the docs that deal with this all the time for thousands like me.

Everything is in place so just like before surgery, I am just waiting things out. My niece Jen and nephew Cody are visiting from Omaha this week so I'll be spending time with them.

The contraptions that are strapped to my chest are getting a little less cumbersome. It's just that they don't move or adjust the way regular breast tissue does, so even though I am sleeping on my sides again, it's not like before. It's an adjustment and it's still weird. At least the pain & pressure is getting better. It just feels like I am wearing a very tight sports bra all the time... and of course I don't have to wear a bra at all anymore!

Celebrating with an open house here on Sunday so I hope to see friends coming by to say hello. I have really enjoyed this duplex I am living in - it's nice to cook and bake goodies and have friends over. Life is good! (Calypso sucks - but life is still good)!

When all else fails, throw a party!

Dec 29, 2013

Continuing on my journey... after yet another visit with yet another doctor on Friday, I found myself asking myself "How am I going to do this?" How will I continue to work? How will I pay these bills? How will I get through this emotionally, physically, and financially? Questions like this can drive you nuts - especially if you are asking yourself because you don't get real sound advice or answers. However, this time I did finally come up with an acceptable answer... "One step at a time."

When I was first diagnosed, I had an attitude of "Oh, it's just Calypso - no biggie." I suppose that was just a bit of denial. Okay, it was a bit of denial and a lot of ignorance. Truth is, I never really paid much attention to what Calypso was really all about and how people dealt with it. I guess we all think "It will never happen to me." I certainly thought that. I really don't know why this happened to me but I don't think it matters.

Jim was diagnosed with pancreatic cancer.... why did that happen to him? He is an athlete and in great shape and no history of cancer in his family. I guess the bottom line is that it's just a crap shoot. So, since it did happen to me, my only option now is to put on my big girl panties and deal with it!

Yes, I have a lot of things to figure out but as I've said all along, I am exceptionally blessed to have the support of great friends. So today I had a party. An open house actually and I invited tons of people, and most of them showed up! It was a bit crowded and noisy at times, but it was exactly what I needed. I just wanted the people here to know how much I appreciate them. And if I could hold a virtual party for all of you out there who have sent prayers my way, I would do that too... just to say thank you to all of you too.

If I were facing this journey alone, I would probably not even venture out the front door. However, knowing that I have so many people taking the journey with me - I could almost say I look forward to it. At least I know if I stumble or fall, a friend will take me by the hand and help me up to continue on our way.

In two days a new year will be upon us. People will be shouting Happy New Year from the rooftops. I am usually tucked into bed asleep when the ball drops. Maybe this year, I will stay up to see it coming and face it head on. One might say that I don't have a lot to look forward to really and yet, I still have that same feeling of a "new year" - a chance to do better.

The majority of my year will be spent having treatments with a grand finale of another surgery. I am probably looking at September or October before it's all said and done. But you know what? That will bring me close to my birthday for one, and for the holidays to roll around again.

My favorite time of year! So, that light at the end of the tunnel will be my focus. I will still take this one step at a time, but I take those steps knowing that I am getting closer to the top of that darn mountain. And once I am up there, it will be me shouting from the mountain top... "Happy New Life!"

Wishing you all the Happiest of New Years - May your dreams come true and your life be blessed!

 # crHappy New Year

Dec 31, 2013

Okay, so I am a little undecided about the New Year. On the one hand, I am always "Happy" to see the new year roll around. Everyone is so optimistic and all about resolutions, a clean slate, etc. Then again, I have a lot of "Crap" to deal with, so I felt it only fair to include the crappy into my greeting.

How nice it would be if I could fast forward to October 2014! I'd have my new permanent boobs, a birthday coming up and all the crap would be behind me. That's not the way life works though, is it? Dealing with the crap makes us appreciate all the non-crappy stuff in our lives. As they say, if it weren't for the darkness, we wouldn't see the stars.

So, as I say good-bye to 2013 and look back I can honestly say I am grateful. I had a great year... enjoyed many hikes, bike rides, zip lines and other outdoor activities with the outdoor group. I only got to climb one 14er this year, but that is one more than I had before and I will be back for more. It's not like they are going anywhere!

I sold my condo and that all went very well. I found a place to rent for now that turned out to be perfect for me. The bunnies are "hoppy" and healthy and getting along fairly well (as long as Wilson minds Daisy). Most of all, I formed many more friendships. The friendships that I had got better and I made new friends as well. There's a saying that goes

"Make new friends, keep the old. One is silver, the other gold." I am blessed with much silver and gold in my life right now.

Now just because I have a lot of crap coming at me in 2014 doesn't mean all is lost. I still plan on doing more hiking and outdoor activities with the group when I can. I will continue to nurture the friendships that I have and always, always be grateful for those special people in my life. Perhaps I should also be grateful for encountering Calypso. If it weren't for this, I may not have really had any idea how many lives I have touched and what wonderful friends I have. Now that is something to be truly grateful for!

As my last journal entry for 2013, I will end with a huge THANK YOU to all who have been taking this journey with me. Whether you are living here in the Springs with me, an online friend, relative or acquaintance I hope you know how much it means to me to have you in my life. I don't ever wish anyone to encounter Calypso however, I do wish for you all to take a moment and count your blessings. They surely outweigh any troubles that come your way.

Wishing you all a Safe, Blessed and Happy New Year.

 # Calypso Wars!

Jan 4, 2014

I know many of you say I am a nice person... always willing to overlook the flaws in others and try to accept things as they are. Well, I am about to show my "dark" side as I share with you a very special letter that I've addressed to "Calypso."

Dear Mr. C,

I know you think you've gotten the best of me. You invaded my breast, which if you weren't aware, is one of a woman's favorite parts. I kinda took that personally. You also tried to sneak a few of your nasty little friends into my lymphatic system but the surgeons rather abruptly showed you all out the door.

Normally I am a "turn the other cheek" type person and forgive easily but as I have learned more about you, I don't think you deserve that. So guess what? I am assembling an army to fight you! Oh, you think with your billions of cells that can multiply so quickly and sneaky are any match for me and my army? I have three words for you: You will lose.

Your measly little cells are no match for the friends I have. I've got love and support and more prayers than you do cells. One other thing I have that you cannot even dare to overcome... FAITH.

Yes, I have decided to tackle you with everything I have. I am even willing to put chemicals in my body to weaken and destroy you. I am willing to radiate my body to make sure there is no trace of you or your horrible friends left in me. I will come back even stronger and wiser than I was before I ever met you and I will be an advocate for others to fight you as well. We will find a cure to wipe you completely out of existence. That may take a bit more time but again, I have faith that we will overcome.

So just know Mr. C that your best days are behind you. You have taken far too many good people from this world and you don't deserve to continue to manifest your ugliness into so many beautiful lives.

Of course you can wave your little white flag, which would be totally out of character for you since you are an ugly, invasive little turd. I just thought it was fair to warn you that you are about to have your ass properly kicked... by a girl!

(not so) Sincerely,

Laura
BED Team
and many, many more supporters that should leave you quaking in your boots!

 # Port-A-Cath 101

Jan 7, 2014

This is one of the educational parts of my journey.

I keep hearing that "Knowledge is power" but you know, before I had this encounter with Calypso, I was more of the mindset that "Ignorance is bliss." At least it is in some cases. Not to say I have been ignorant, but this is not the type of education I ever expected to gain. I just like the simple life - to enjoy it and share it and try to make things a little better out there in the world. Then Calypso had to come along and complicate the hell out of things!

So, in sharing this journey with you all I thought I would educate you on a port, or port-a-cath, or med-port. There are several names for it. I had one put in my chest today. The device allows blood draws and the chemo meds to be administered without poking the vein every time. The chemo drugs are really harsh and can damage smaller veins. The port is about the size of a quarter. It is snaked through and connected to one of the larger veins so that the meds are diluted and absorbed quickly into the blood stream. The port has a silicone covering so it can be injected hundreds of times and not be damaged. Pretty cool little device... worth googling if you feel so inclined.

So surgery went well today and relatively short compared to the last time. They tried to put the port in sub-clavian on both the right and the left side, but apparently my veins were being un-cooperative so they went for the jugular! The port itself is on my chest wall but the line runs up the right inner jugular vein. Now I have my chemo class on Friday and the chemical invasion begins on Wednesday next week.

Here is a photo of me after surgery today. Hope you all find this as fascinating as I do!

Port-a-bility

Jan 9, 2014

Just back from a hike at Palmer Park on this lovely Colorado sunny afternoon! After a week of hospitals, appointments, procedures and NO sunshine it felt so good to get outside. Part of the healing process is to take care of me and staying active and getting some exercise is a huge part of that. I need to do more of this to build up my strength to kick some Calypso butt. I was able to take the bandages off today from the port, so I don't feel like I am wearing a three pound collar!

Tomorrow I have an echocardiogram, lab work and chemo class. That should be the last of the pre-chemo checklist. I was originally scheduled to return to work on Monday but with chemo starting I will be extending a few more weeks. I hope to do well enough to get back to work at least part-time. I was more productive when I was working!

Saturday I am going snow tubing with the Outdoor Group. I asked my Oncology Surgeon if it was okay and she kind of made a funny face and deferred the decision to the plastic surgeon. When I asked him, he made the exact same face and said probably not the best idea but that I couldn't really hurt the contraptions if I fell on them. The only concern was if I pulled my arms one way or the other and too much strain that could damage them. The port is not a problem or concern. I guess I will have to just use my best judgment when I get there. The plastic surgeon did say that if I went I would probably just be sore afterwards. How that is different than feeling like I am wearing a super tight sports bra 24/7, I don't know!

I just know that Colorado is such a great place and winter is no longer a season that I dread. I love winter activities!

I will be back out there soon, starting snowball fights (and blaming someone else) and hiking in the snow. It will take more than a bit of Calypso to keep me off the trails!

Hope the New Year is off to a great start for everyone. I'm ready to get the show on the road... stare this beast down and put it in its place!

Chemo class - did I pass?

Jan 10, 2014

Chemo class today... talk about an education! I can sum it up in one word... overwhelming. At least there wasn't a test at the end!

I have several nurses and a pharmacist available to me during this process. As reassuring as that is, the list of who to call, when to call, symptoms to look for, side effects to expect, medications to take, etc.... that is the overwhelming part! Lots of handouts, brochures to look through and a few freebies like lotions, pillows and knit hats thrown in for good measure. We took a walk through the hospital over to the infusion lab to see where I check in and where the actual treatment facility is. I have to say everyone we encountered was so nice and helpful. I have a lot of respect for these people that do this work, day in and day out. In my short career in the medical field, I learned that it takes a very special person to sign up for this type of work.

So, after the overdose of information we decided a nice lunch and afternoon of shopping was in order. That was a good distraction but by the time I got home I was tired. This stuff can wear me out as much as a long hike up a mountain!

As has become the "norm" for me - I did break down and cry later. This was partly because I was just tired and overwhelmed, but also because I read so many wonderful things online from friends. I get text messages and emails and cards in the mail to remind me that I am not alone in this journey. So the tears are a mix of being scared, anxious, grateful and overwhelmed. I told my sister that when your head fills up with so much information, something has to leak out through your eyeballs!

So, once that is all out of my system I am able to think clear headed again. I keep circling back to the fact that I have so very many supporters and I can't help but think "nobody should have to do this alone." I know change is coming and not just the chemo, Calypso, new boobs, etc. I know when all of this is done I will be looking at a career change. I know it will be something to do with helping others... perhaps in the health care industry. I have plenty of time to sort it all out, but I am now thinking it may be to help others who have nobody else. Of all the types of Calypso, we are the lucky ones. There is so much support available. Perhaps my calling will be for another type of disease or illness or assistance to those in need. It's going to be a very interesting year that's for sure. 2014 will be one to remember and a turning point in my life.

I will keep looking for clues and signs. I know I am being shown a new trail to follow and it may lead to a mountain taller than any I have climbed thus far. Finding my way.... requires nothing but faith and awareness.

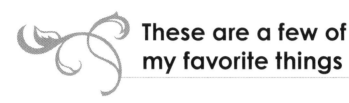

These are a few of my favorite things

Jan 11, 2014

Raindrops on roses and whiskers on bunnies are wonderful, but tonight some of my favorite things are my affirmations. In preparing for C-day I have been going through some of the online posts that I've shared and decided to put some of them here.

* Hardships often prepare ordinary people for an extraordinary destiny.
* Physical strength is measured by what we can carry. Inner strength is measured by what we can bear.
* Faith: It doesn't make things easy. It makes them possible.
* Life doesn't get easier; you just get stronger.
* A strong positive mental attitude will create more miracles than any wonder drug.
* Happiness comes when we stop complaining about the troubles we have and thank God for the troubles we don't have.
* Laughter gives you reason to hope. Tears give you reason to fight.
* The struggle you are in today is developing the strength you need for tomorrow. Don't give up!
* What doesn't kill you only makes you stronger.

*   When something bad happens, you have three choices:
    You can let it define you
    You can let it destroy you
    Or you can let is strengthen you.

*   I believe in the power of prayer, the energy of love, the strength of faith and the will of a determined person to carry on and act with these until they make it through.

Now that I've shared some of my favorites, I will invite you to share your favorite affirmation, quote, bible verse, etc. and post them here. I will keep these and read them as I am getting chemo this week and the following weeks. I've had some meltdown moments recently but now I am feeling my strength building again and gaining momentum, so let's keep it rolling!

I am strong. I am invincible. I am woman! (Now there's a throwback)!

Thank you all - your support and prayers mean everything to me.

****

Adding on.....

 From Mary C:
* And He will raise you up on eagle's wings, bear you on the breath of dawn, make you to shine like the sun, and hold you in the palm of His hand.
~Michael Joncas

From Marie:
* We either make ourselves miserable, or we make ourselves strong. The amount of work is the same.
— Carlos Castaneda

And one of my favorites that I can't believe I didn't include in the original:

* Psalms 23:1-6~
The LORD is my Shepherd, I shall not want.
He makes me lie down in green pastures,
He leads me beside quiet waters, He restores my soul.
He guides me in paths of righteousness for His name's sake.
Even though I walk through the valley of the shadow of death,
I will fear no evil, for You are with me;
Your rod and Your staff, they comfort me.
You prepare a table before me in the presence of my enemies.
You anoint my head with oil; my cup overflows.
Surely goodness and love will follow me all the days of my life,
And I will dwell in the house of the LORD forever.
Amen.

By Kate
Suscipe of Catherine McAuley-Foundress of the Sisters of Mercy

My God I am yours for time and eternity. Teach me to cast myself entirely into the arms of Your loving providence with the most lively, unlimited confidence in Your compassionate, tender pity. Grant me, o most merciful redeemer, that whatever You ordain or permit may be acceptable to me. (that's the hardest line) Take from my heart all painful anxiety; suffer nothing to sadden me but sin; nothing to delight me but the hope of coming to the possession of YOU, my God and my all, in Your everlasting kingdom. Amen.

I say that with my students before every class every day.

By Dawn S
* What doesn't kill you only makes you stronger except BEARS! Bears will kill ya." LOL!!!!

"Courage makes everything look different."

"Triumph - umpf added to TRY."

"God doesn't promise a comfortable journey only a safe landing."

"You cannot climb uphill by thinking downhill thoughts."

"Challenges make you discover things about yourself that you never really knew." Cicely Tyson

"There is no such thing as a problem that doesn't have a gift in it".

"To change your attitude is to change your life."

"Friendship fills up a lot of little ruts in the road."

By Amy
The one that resonates with me is: "What if you woke up tomorrow with the things you were thankful (thanked God) for today". This always reminds me to not take the things in my life for granted. I included the "going to church" and "not going to church" versions :) The meaning resonates regardless, I think...

By Anne P
"Inch by inch, life's a cinch. Yard by yard, life is hard." Remember Bison Peak: Your own inner strength, friends pushing you on when you were physically and emotionally spent, and a goal that made it all worthwhile.

By Danni
This is the day the Lord has made. We will rejoice and be glad in it. - Ps. 118:24 This is how I begin my day every day because this is the first thing I see on the wall plaque in my bedroom! I got a calendar in the mail at work that had some really cool affirmation statements on it. A few of yours are on it, but this one is another I think I am going to subscribe to: "I take nothing for granted. I now have only good days or great days." I pray for you continually, Laura-la! Know that I and many others you don't know are with you in this Calypso fight! You are strong and invincible!

This is a rock that Laura and Craig saw on a hike. They wanted to bring it to me but said it was probably about 200 pounds and several feet in diameter. Well, it's the thought that counts and this huge heart makes me feel a whole lotta love!

Pennies from Heaven

Jan 13, 2014

Over the past few days I have found several pennies on the ground (face up of course). I am thinking this is a good sign!

I've got my fighting spirit back too!!! Can you hear the "Rocky" music? Eye of the Tiger... GRRRRRR!!!! I'm sure it has to do with my getting out and hiking/walking the past few days. I missed quite a bit of time last week with appointments, procedures and the surgery so now I am back on track.

I'd like to thank all who sent me affirmations, bible verses and quotes after my last post. There are so many wonderful things to think of while I am getting chemo. I have much to be grateful for and friends and family are right there at the top of the list. You have no idea how much it means to me to have you along on the journey.

A post online from yesterday:

"It's your road and yours alone. Others may walk it with you but no one can walk it for you."

While this may be true, I certainly don't feel alone at all. Every time I log on to the Caring Bridge and see how many visits and hearts I have it just makes me smile... and sometimes brings a tear to my eye. If I could bottle up the feeling and sell it, I would be a kazillionnaire! Everyone should feel so loved at least once in his or her lifetime.

So I have everything prepared for Wednesday. Who knew so much planning went in to getting a few chemicals injected into your body? Believe me, it's information overload on a regular basis! My chemo bag includes things like snacks, wipes, tissues, water, mints, thermometer, first aid kit, meds, etc. For a while there I thought I was going to need a roller bag! Oh, and of course my day-timer that has all of my affirmations in it. I may also bring the cards that have come in the mail and read them again. I ask you... How could things NOT go well with this kind of preparation and support?

I get lab work tomorrow to make sure we can attain "lift off" for Wednesday. Then on Thursday I go in for a shot (I was hoping Tequila - but no) of a drug called Neulasta to boost my white blood cell count. I get 14 days between chemo so we'll see how this one goes.

That's what is on the menu for this week. Thank you again for all your support, love and prayers. I have a good feeling about this!

# It's no little thing

Jan 14, 2014

Tomorrow is C-Day... and that C does not stand for Chocolate (darn it)! Wouldn't that be awesome though if Chocolate were the cure for Calypso? Ah... if only!

I tried to get to bed early but I'm not sure that I'll get a good night's sleep. Not that I am worried really but it's like any day that something major is happening in your life... there's much anticipation.

I have my affirmations printed and taking them with me. On top of that I got a card in the mail today from my friend Cindy. It was so amazingly appropriate that I must share.

The card reads: "Life is hard sometimes - crazy, mixed up, messed up. And there you are in the middle of it all, just doing your thing... being strong and brave and beautiful, like it's no big deal."

"But let me tell you girl, not everyone can do what you can do. Not everyone can handle things the way you can. While you wonder sometimes if you are doing ok... the rest of us are just watching you in wonder."

That brought such a smile to my face... and to get that the day before this journey gets tough was amazing timing. It occurs to me that many of us do these little things like drop a card in the mail, call a friend for no reason, smile or say hello to a stranger passing by. We do these little things without realizing sometimes the impact that we have on the other person. Isn't it nice to imagine that your card or phone call or smile may have just made someone's day? It might have been the only good or positive thing in their day.

Just as this card made my day and was so appropriate. I actually do not feel like I am all that amazing, strong or beautiful. But it's nice to know that someone else thinks so. I know I've been doing the best I can with what I have control over (which is actually NONE of this). I know I am feeling positive and strong and I have "good vibrations" going. I have the power of prayer and my faith. I have well wishes from friends and family near and far. I just don't see a down side here. So whether it's me, or just the circumstances that I have been blessed to be in perhaps I can feel strong, brave and beautiful.

Thank you all for walking along this far. I hope you will continue the journey with me. Just like those footprints in the sand... when things get really difficult is when God picks us up and carries us along.

I'll post an update tomorrow and give you all an education on chemo... that has to leave you all on the edge of your seats. Kind of like the soap opera with the dramatic music at the end... stay tuned until next time!

 # Day one is done

Jan 15, 2014

After much discussion, preparation, decisions and soul searching about what is the right path for me to take I successfully completed round one of chemotherapy.

Thus the score stands:

Laura - 1
Calypso - 0
He ain't gonna like the next three rounds cuz I am gonna whoop his ass again! (pardon my French).

Today was actually a good experience. Eva and Bobbie went with me to the Doctors appointment at 8:30am then we headed over to the infusion center and got the show on the road. My nurse, Kim was wonderful. Everyone was really wonderful actually and I did very well. Bobbie stayed for a bit then left and Dawn arrived for a short visit right after her, so I was in good company with my BED team.

They have warm blankets, heated seats on the recliner; TV, snacks, drinks and they fed me lunch. Not too shabby for a newbie, huh? I did have my own Star Wars blanket this time, made by my two nieces Victoria and Sammy. I will probably just opt for their warm blankets next time and save this one for special occasions. I visited some, read a little and napped a little. Afterwards, Eva and I took a short walk around the park and then she brought me home. I went for another short walk then too.

They did give me IV steroids and I also have some pills to take for three days. I wasn't crazy about that but if it helps me to stay ahead of any nausea I'll do it. The first chemo drug they gave had a cover over it that was brown... you know, like "milk chocolate" brown? For a moment I thought perhaps they did discover that chocolate cures Calypso! The drug is light sensitive so they had to cover it. It was actually a red-orange color, which left the same color in the toilet. Eva and I thought Sammie would probably be interested to know this. LOL

I am including a "selfie" taken just before we got started. The port site has been a bit tender but posed no problems today. These two drugs will be administered every two weeks and three more rounds. Then I get to the next drug, which will be weekly. If any Springs locals want to accompany me to chemo sessions, let me know. I may get to the point where I can drive myself but it's nice to have someone there with me.

Thank you all for the prayers and positive thoughts today. They obviously worked like a charm!

Love and hugs to all.

The port is behaving well so I am all hooked up and ready for my first infusion here.

 # Give Forward

Jan 17, 2014

I have to say that I have the best little sister in the world. Even if she weren't my sister, she would still be my friend. Eva set up a website for a fundraiser for me during this battle. You all know how expensive weapons can be!

I am fortunate to have health insurance but the HSA account will only carry me so far and I have a long road to go. I am not even caught up with 2013 medical bills and now 2014 bills are rolling in.

It is totally out of my nature to ask for assistance in this way, but I have been reassured by several friends that there are people who want to help and either don't know how or are unable to help in any other way. So I agreed to the fundraiser. It's a humbling experience to be in this position, as most of you know how independent I am. I am the one who normally plays the role of giver, not taker.

There are resources out there for financial assistance. I've been able to take advantage of a few but I am in a middle ground... I make enough money to support myself pretty well yet too much to qualify for much assistance. I have heard stories of others who have gone through this under much worse circumstances so I want you all to know that I do intend to also give forward after my battle is won and to help others in their Calypso battles. I know much more than I did before all of this began and hope to help others to find these resources and to know they are not alone.

I have been so blessed to have so many supporters sending love, prayers and hugs my way. So let me just say up front... THANK YOU to all of you who have been taking this journey with me and for keeping my spirits up. My strength comes from my faith in God and from loved ones like you. God bless you all.

 # Here's how I "C" things

Jan 19, 2014

The way I "C" it
C is what the year 2014 is to me.
This year of Calypso is also one of...
Change
Challenge
Courage
Chemo
and yes, a little Crying too.

And the year also brings...
Cheer
Caring
Comfort
and of course my favorite C word... CHOCOLATE!

Though I have to say one of the most unusual things has been happening to me the past few days - I am not craving chocolate much lately. This could be the worst side effect yet!

I am so very fortunate to have NOT had any side effects from the first round of chemo. I am taking some anti-nausea meds when needed, but otherwise you would never know by looking at me that I have undergone chemo.

I mean, come on - look at this photo from today's hike at the Garden of the Gods. How can Calypso even compete with my supporters and me on such a lovely day? I can only hope that the next few rounds go as well.

Here I am with Allison, Renee, Connie, Dalene & Les at the Siamese Twins.

I do believe that (besides my faith and support system) sunshine and fresh air every day have played a huge part in my well-being. I've done a lot of research on chemo and the effects on the body and I don't have to tell you that it is some nasty, scary stuff! One piece of advice I took to heart was to hydrate plenty in the first 24-48 hours and to get out and walk every day. Seems to be working for me, so I think I'll keep it up.

Next round is January 29th... ring side seats are available now so get 'em while they last and watch me kick Calypso all the way out the door! It's guaranteed to be a knock out!

Is it really chemo or is it just me?

Jan 21, 2014

Tomorrow will mark the one-week post-chemo treatment and today was the first day I did not take ANY anti-nausea meds. How weird is that? I guess I'm not sure if I need to just take them and stay ahead of it or do a "wait and see" type thing. I am not usually one to take pills for whatever ails me so this is all new to me.

I am feeling good - walking/hiking every day and hydrating. I guess that is the key because most days I feel quite normal (though my sister would tell you I've never been normal). I wonder if it really was chemo they had in those bags? Maybe I shouldn't press my luck and just keep my mouth shut. Of course, that is very unlike me as well.

So, my new ringtone on my phone is Tubthumping by Chumbawumba. Some of you may have to look that up. Even though it's more of a drinking song, I like the phrase "I get knocked down, but I get up again. You're never gonna keep me down!" I imagine myself with boxing gloves on and punching Calypso while I sing this. Nice visual, isn't it?

I had a lymphedema assessment today. More interesting and educational things are coming my way. They took 22 lymph nodes out when they did the mastectomy. Normal in the axillary area is about 25-30 so I have very few left and those guys really need to step up to the plate! I can get along with very few as long as I train these guys to compensate and pick up the slack for their parted companions. Everything looks good or "normal" with just some tenderness and tightness in the upper arm. I was given some exercises to stretch and strengthen the upper body and arms. My little soldiers are going to boot camp starting tomorrow morning! I figure if I am going to be showing off the new ta-ta's this summer I will need to have good arms to match. Hello 70's - are halter tops still in style?

So, I am continuing to have good days and keeping my spirits up. You know, despite all that has happened thus far I can still smile and say "Life is Good." It's never perfect, even for perfectly healthy people... but it is good.

Thank you all again and again for your support and encouragement. I am feeling especially blessed to see that our fundraiser is growing so I can relax and not stress so much over these medical bills. It's difficult to ask for help and I was just telling a friend of mine that it's okay to ask for help and it's okay to be the receiver sometimes. I am practicing what I preach now at least!

Blessings to all and good night!

My cup runneth over

Jan 22, 2014

You've all seen the movie "The Grinch that stole Christmas" right? So, if you can picture the scene near the end when his heart grows so large that is breaks the frame you will have an idea of how I am feeling tonight.

I can also relate to the movie "It's a Wonderful Life" yet again because I truly am living the George Bailey life right now.... you know the part after he gets to see what things would be like if he'd never been born and realizes just how many friends he has? Yep, that's me.

I am so overwhelmed by the generosity of the people in my life... both from my past and the present. I have been so blessed from the start to have friends and family rally around me and offer support and prayers and now once again in my hour of need, there you all are.

It doesn't matter what I write or how many ways I can find to say thank you, it will never seem like enough. This is not something I will ever forget or take for granted. My only wish is to be given the opportunity to pay it forward when someone else is in need.

I am reading a book that talks about the 12 Laws of Karma. Like me, I'm sure you were not aware that there was more to Karma, did you? It's not about rewards and punishment either. One part in particular that I liked talks about how important it is to allow others to help you. I have always enjoyed volunteering my time and helping others. It's not entirely a selfless act because it does leave you feeling good. According to this law of karma, if you don't allow others to also help you, then you are denying them that same joy that you feel. I never really looked at it that way and it was so difficult for me to ask for help. Now that I have experienced this first hand, I understand how it works and completes the circle. There must surely be an overdose of joy going on right now.

My life has definitely been changed by the events of the past few months. I did not comprehend just how much this would affect the rest of my life and I have a feeling I am just beginning to scratch the surface. But I know for certain that it's all for the best and that my life is changing for the better.

Thank you again and again for your support, your generosity and most of all for accompanying me on this journey. Though I don't yet know the destination, I know that the journey is what is important right now.

In heartfelt gratitude...

Get well cards and "Rocks for Recovery"

Easy does it

Jan 26, 2014

I guess I had a gentle reminder last night that I am in fact NOT Superwoman. I took a hike with some friends Saturday morning, which ended up being about three hours worth. It was nothing strenuous but there was a mix of ice, snow, mud and sunshine. After all, this is Colorado! I came home and napped in the afternoon so I could go to the Luau last night. Yes, you read that right. A Luau. In Colorado. In January. I have the best friends you know!

I took it easy at the party and didn't stay long, no alcohol - just had a few bites to eat and visited. Perhaps it was something I ate because I ended up being rather ill throughout the night. I suspect a mild case of food poisoning but can't be sure. I had to cancel my hike today and pretty much lay around and do nothing. It was such a beautiful day too - sunny and 50's.

So, that made me realize that I am not Superwoman. Guess I had to come to that conclusion eventually - though I never tire of everyone telling me how good I look. Just because I don't have super powers doesn't mean I am weak though. Sometimes the body just has to get your attention when you think you are invincible and make you slow down a bit.

After taking a day off, I am feeling better and will surely be up and about tomorrow and definitely ready for my next show down with Mr. C. That is on Wednesday and I am ready. Round two will surely be another knock out!

Until then I just keep that "Rocky" tune going through my head... Eye of the Tiger baby!

Tough choices

Jan 28, 2014

I've had some tough choices to make over the past 2-3 months. Some came easy and others I struggled with. I don't exactly have a history of making great choices but then how many of us really do?

Our choices are what shape us into who we are. We make choices based on what we know and what we need at the time. Good choices usually make us happy and bad choices teach us lessons. Either way, we all have to learn to live with the choices we make since many of them cannot be re-done. I have second, third and fourth guessed my decisions to do chemo. After revisiting the numbers that show hormone therapy reduces the chance of recurrence more than chemo I questioned my decision to proceed. This was a temporary pause only as I was reminded that chemo is what kills those microscopic cells that may be lingering in my body. Also, I made these decisions because I want to do everything possible to increase my chances of survival. That's what it basically comes down to.

So, as I was talking to Bobbie tonight we had a little chuckle over the choice of having children. Kelly and I had compared cancer to pregnancy previously and so we decided that cancer doesn't look all that bad in comparison.

Children will cause you pain... from the day they are born. Pregnancy makes you sick and vomiting and feeling like crap for months. Not to mention all the weird foods you crave (as I write this I am eating peanut butter and jelly on a tortilla followed by a popsicle). Kids will cause you many sleepless nights, make you pull your hair out, sick with worry and regrets. See? Not a lot of difference! And as Kelly said - at least the chemo & radiation will end in a few months!

So, yes I am joking about this of course. Children are wonderful - sugar and spice and all that jazz. Just because I never had any doesn't mean I can't appreciate them. I actually can appreciate them more because I get to be the awesome Aunt and spoil them, and then send them home! (parents aren't liking me right now, but grandparents know exactly what I am talking about)!

Choices... just like my choice to make the most of my journey with Calypso. I choose to stay positive and look at the bright side. Yes, there are bright sides... of course the new ta-ta's are the biggest "perk" though not the easiest way to obtain them! And breast cancer is one of the most survivable cancers out there. I have also had the joy of seeing how many friends and family members care about me. So, yes I am the lucky one.

I tend to look at life this way, not just since I developed this disease. There is always someone out there who has it much worse than I do. I've mentioned my friend with pancreatic cancer. My little problem is very insignificant in comparison.

So, my choice is to carry on, be strong and come out a winner. Next round of chemo is tomorrow. I choose to live, laugh and love! Who is with me?

# Round two and another knock out!

Jan 30, 2014

Round two of chemo yesterday and I have to declare another knock out. Mr. C put up a slight struggle more than last time but it was once again "easy peasy lemon squeezy!"

It's actually quite a nice environment. I still feel like I don't belong there because I feel so healthy and good. Almost makes me feel guilty. I make jokes with the nurses and staff. I'm sure before this is all over we'll be BFF's or something like that! It sure takes some special people to do this kind of work day after day and be so upbeat and kind. After my short career in the medical field I do have a new appreciation for that line of work. It is certainly more than I had in me at the time!

So upon arrival yesterday I was given a warm blanket, a drink and reclined my chair to settle in for some fluids. Eva picked me up and we met Dawn and Bobbie at the Doctors office first and met with the Nurse Practitioner to go over my labs and make sure I was doing okay. I've been very lucky to have so few side effects and so far the hair is still intact. I expect that will change in the next week or so... unless I am that rare percentage that doesn't lose the hair?

I think my only complaint if you can call it that is that I do tire easily. That can be frustrating to me but hardly even worth mentioning really.

About two hours after I arrived, I was served lunch then had a nap and before you know it I am done and ready to go home. Oh and I had to get a chest X-ray because my right clavicle bone is protruding. Not sure what happened or how but the X-ray showed nothing so I'm not sure what they will do next. It's been this way since the port surgery but I thought it was just swelling - except it hasn't gone away.

Went back today for a shot called Neulasta. This helps boost my White Blood Cell count and it's obviously working because my labs showed a pretty high number this time!

So, that's round two summary. I have two more rounds of this cycle every other week then we start cycle 2 on a weekly basis. I hope to return to work late February and probably part time since I will be having a chemo day once a week. I have been keeping busy but a little out of sorts having to think what day of the week it is all the time. Every day is Saturday to me!

So the score stands:
Laura - 2
Calypso - big fat zero!
He has no idea how competitive I am, does he?

Hair Today, Gone Tomorrow

Feb 1, 2014

The day finally arrived and right on time. They say you will start losing your hair 2-3 weeks after starting chemo. Today is 17 days from my first treatment. I could have done without the promptness, thank you!

I'm not to the worst part yet. I have so darn much hair that it will probably take another week or two for it to all fall out. I will however cut it super short so it's not such a shock to see a wad of hair anytime I run my fingers through it. That will make it easier on the drains in the shower too.

So, one good thing to come out of this phase... about 10 days ago I went to the DMV to update my drivers license. My address was out of date and I was loving my hair style, so I figured this would be a good time to take care of that. Well, as timing would have it on this day when I noticed my hair coming out in large quantities, I get my new drivers license in the mail and I am pretty happy with the photo - see attached. At least I have that, right?

So yes, I did shed a few tears along with the hair, but you know the great thing about hair? It grows back!

Laura Janca

I am thinking that maybe Sinead O'Connor had a good thing going though. There's very little "muss or fuss" about baldness. Perhaps I will take on a "Kojak" persona, stock up on some lollipops and walk around saying "Who loves you baby?"

I've picked up a few hats and scarves and may even consider a wig. I just need to decide if I want to be a sassy blonde or a saucy redhead. Any input from ya'all on that?

I'll post a photo again after the cut and what the heck, I will do a baldy one too. Just to give you all something to look forward to.

Short timer

Feb 2, 2014

The next step came sooner than I expected but I understand now why chemo patients cut or shave their heads when the hair starts to fall out. It's a little unnerving to see a wad of hair in your hands when you simply brush your hair back or to see hairs all over your shirt every time you get dressed. So I did the deed and chopped it off.

I went to Great Clips down the street and managed to tell the stylist what was going on without choking up. She was very sweet - wearing a #7 Bronco Jersey too. After I told her I wanted it short she told me that they do free chemo cuts. How about them apples? Thank you Jennifer!

I also asked her to save my hair - being the sentimental sap that I am lately, she gently laid it into my lap as she cut. It was a great experience. And the more she cut, the more I liked it. I thought it would be really hard but this cut is funky and sassy. We left just enough of the highlights in to make it interesting. I can't decide if I look like Kelly or my mother. Either way, that's a good thing!

I did something else for myself today. I joined 24 Hour Fitness. They have monthly plans and no contracts, so I thought it would behoove me to sign up (and I wanted to use that word - behoove). They have a small pool that will help with my arm rehab and getting full range of motion, and on days when I can't get out to walk, I can hit the treadmill. Nothing is going to stand in the way of me kicking Calypso butt. Are you hearing that Rocky theme music again? Me too!

So, today was a good day. This week is my "off" week of chemo so I plan to enjoy it - even though the weather isn't cooperating. More snow in the forecast. But who cares? Life is good! Calypso still sucks but Life is Good!

# It's my party and I'll cry if I want to!

Feb 5, 2014

You would cry too if it happened to you.

I've been doing a lot of this lately. It's not always a bad thing either. I looked outside this morning to see my neighbor shoveling my driveway... and then came the tears. How very kind of them.

I decided to not join the gym today so I went over to cancel and as I left... then came the tears. This decision was more due to my immune system being compromised and the more I thought about being in a gym with sweaty bodies and sharing locker rooms, pool, etc. was probably not a good choice.

My emotions have been highly sensitive lately. I hesitated to even write a journal today because I try very hard to stay positive but after finally breaking down and calling my BFF Kelly she assured me that I had every right to have a down day anytime I wanted to. Of course, she had me laughing again by the time we hung up too. You know, after 33 years I guess she knows me best (besides my family of course)!

So, after having myself a nice little pity party today (sorry for those who were not invited) I know I can pick myself up by the bootstraps (if I were wearing boots) and get back on track. What's that saying again? If it weren't for the darkness, you wouldn't see the stars?

I am excited for the Olympics to start tomorrow. I invited a few girlfriends over to watch the opening ceremonies. I am always just in awe of watching these athletes who work and train so hard and so long to be their best and make the team. With the Olympic Training Center here in the Springs I guess it's easier than ever to catch Olympic fever! And the timing is perfect... I will go back to work on February 24th - right after it's over. I rarely watch TV these days but for the next two weeks, the tube will be on pretty much non-stop.

Oh yeah and watching the stories of the athletes in the Olympics tonight... you guessed it - then came the tears!

Thanks for indulging me on this journal... and if you call me or see me and give me a hug and my eyes start to water, just know that it's only because I feel all the love and support from family and friends and my cup runneth over!

Now, time to soldier on....

Kill 'em with Kindness!

Feb 8, 2014

I had a good outing today at Barr Lake State Park for the Bald Eagle viewing. We had a group of 11 great folks from the Outdoor Club. Though I just did a short walk (2.5 miles) it was great to get outside and we did see one eagle high up in the trees across the lake. There were plenty of binoculars and cameras to zoom in on him. They also did a presentation at the Visitors center with one of those gorgeous guys so we could get up close and personal.

They even had a few "props" as shown here. I look vicious, don't I? Well, I certainly can be when it comes to fighting Calypso! Bring it on baby!

This week was such a mix... starting out cold and snowing lots, which meant I couldn't get outside for my exercise much. I was also snacking more on sweets so I do believe this is why I was feeling so lousy on Wednesday. I got my act together later in the week and out to hike Friday & Saturday. Feeling much better now and ready to kick more Calypso butt!

Round three is scheduled for Wednesday. The photo here will give Calypso an idea of what is in store. Yeah, that's right, this is what is left of the eagle that came after me, so you better watch out - I've got my fighting spirit back so don't mess with me! I feel another knock-out coming around!

My fundraiser is going well. I still have a long road ahead but again, knowing I have so much love, support and prayers coming in, it makes the journey that much easier for me. You all have surpassed my expectations in your generosity and kindness.

If you are unable to make a donation, just pay it forward in kindness. I have discovered that the more I search for kindness in the world, the more I find it. It is everywhere. So, as Ellen says on her show every day... please be kind to one another. Instead of losing your temper at someone who cuts you off in traffic, just smile and give them room. You can bet they aren't going to stress over what they just did, so why should you?

Next time you are at any type of customer service desk, getting "less than" customer service - try smiling and telling them to have a nice day when you are done. It will probably throw them off a bit but maybe, just maybe they will "get it" and pass it on. Life is so much nicer when we spread a little kindness around. Better yet, spread a LOT of kindness around. It's not like you can run out of it, right? I promise you will feel better the more you do it.

Thanks again for following, indulging my writings, sending prayers & love and most of all for your support. I can feel myself being lifted up right now!

As promised, here is my "baldy" shot, except I wasn't completely bald. I was more like a "fuzzy" gal here. It was really weird cutting it. I didn't want to shave it so I just grabbed the scissors and cut it down as far as I could, kind of giggling the entire time! I mean how often in life would anyone actually do this? It was fun!

Hello Chemo, Hello Dolly!

Feb 13, 2014

What a roller coaster ride this week was. I started out on Monday volunteering at Hospice for a couple hours in the morning. I can't see patients while I am doing chemo so I try to get in a few hours in the office whenever I can. I am going back to work soon (part time) so I figured this would also test my stamina and my ability to think. I have what is called "chemo brain" so I have my moments. Suffice it to say I write a lot of things down now!

I got home and started feeling chilled and tired so I took a hot shower and a long nap. Later than night I was running a low grade fever so I called the on call Doc and got permission to take Tylenol. I had no other symptoms at that time. Tuesday I still felt puny but it was a nice day and I thought a walk would do me good so I met a friend at the park and did a nice, easy walk - about 3.5 miles. It felt good to be out and seemed to help.... until I got back in the car to get home. Feeling very tired I made it home and took another hot shower. Dawn took me to get my labs drawn since I didn't feel like I should drive feeling this way. I was still feeling chilled and had a fever too. When I got home, I took another hot shower, went to bed and stayed there all night. Bobbie came over and fixed me dinner then I fell asleep on her. I was sweating bullets by this time so I knew the fever was breaking.

Wednesday morning I woke up feeling okay and no fever! Seems it was just a 24-hour bug of some kind because I went to my Doctor appointment and got my chemo. The Nurse Practitioner did tell me that my "short" 3.5 mile walk might have been a little too much so I should cut it down. I told her that was cutting it down for me! Still, I suppose on days I am not feeling well, I should go really slower. There will be plenty of time for my longer, more difficult hikes once this is all over. Those mountains aren't going anywhere (though I am certain they miss me as much as I miss them)!

All went well, actually feeling better all day long. That's good because Dawn and my other friend Laura had got tickets for us to see Hello Dolly at the Pikes Peak Center that night! Laura picked me up and we had dinner, then the show - a perfect girls night out. I can't thank them enough. It was a memorable night.

As a matter of fact I still think I am so blessed that I have such caring friends to help me along this journey. I hope none of you feel like you are doing too little or not enough. I enjoy every text, email, card and phone call. I appreciate the rides to appointments, walks & hikes, visits and words of encouragement. For those of you further away, I know you keep me in your prayers and that makes all the difference in the world! And those who helped by contributing to my fundraiser... WOW! That took a huge burden off of my shoulders and I can't thank you enough. Please know that you ARE all helping me along in my journey and that every gesture is very much appreciated!

Looking forward to some nice weather this weekend after that bit of winter we just had. I think that's the coldest I've seen it since I moved here. Fortunately it doesn't usually last long. I am going to the Denver Botanic Gardens for the Orchid Showcase on Saturday. We went last year and got so many beautiful photos. Again - very blessed to have friends who keep me encouraged and uplifted!

Thank you all for everything you do. You've made this journey so much more bearable for me and I know I will see it through to the end. After all... "I get by with a little help from my friends!"

God Bless.

At the Denver Botanic Gardens taking hundreds of photos.
Here's a spoiler: I went to the ER this same night… read on!

A minor bump in the road but it's in the rearview mirror now!

Feb 20, 2014

If you are wondering why I haven't written anything in over a week, well let me tell you. I made what I thought would be a short trip to the ER on Saturday because my left breast was red and very angry looking. I also had a low-grade fever. After five days in the hospital, many rounds of antibiotics and surgery to remove that angry breast, I am back home.

Eva took me to the ER Saturday night and they started me on some very powerful antibiotics every 12 hours. They wanted to keep me overnight for observation. I realize now what a good decision that was. After 5-6 rounds of these super antibiotics the redness continued to spread and fevers accompanied. My plastic surgeon made the call to remove the temporary filler. So on Tuesday afternoon, out it came along with a lot of puss. Don't mean to gross you out but those are the facts. We are still unsure of how the infection started but with my immune system being suppressed it doesn't take much for bacteria to take advantage.

After many blood cultures, I was told I had Staphylococcus Aureus. This bacteria gets in to the blood stream and one of its favorite targets is foreign objects. The ID (Infectious Disease) Doc says it's a 'sticky' bacteria so we will be doing IV antibiotics for 2-4 weeks before resuming chemo.

We are watching the other breast and the port closely to make sure they don't fall under attack as well. Just to clarify, this was not MRSA - the resistant kind of bacteria. I would probably still be in the hospital if it were. This one is labeled MSSA (the sensitive kind) and has responded to the antibiotics.

I have also hit almost bottom on my white count, which makes me Neutropenic. Notice how my vocabulary has improved since I encountered Calypso? So for the next few days I need to be very careful coming into contact with others and what foods I eat. Hopefully my white count will come back up soon. Next labs will be done on Wednesday (my previously scheduled 4th round of chemo).

How's that for an exciting week? It wasn't easy that's for sure but again, my BED team pulled me through it along with many, many friends and family sending prayers. The nurses at Memorial Hospital deserve kudos as well. They were all just the best. One of my favorites had to be Linda - a former NYC cop. She is Puerto Rican or as she calls herself, New Yorican! What a hoot. She sure made my stay bearable and dare I say fun at times? I am so fortunate to continue to be surrounded by such amazing people.

My return to work will be extended to late March. I'm not sure I will remember how to do my job at this point. My Team Leader has been awesome too and helped me through the process of Disability/FMLA.

That's about it from here. Glad to be home and sleep in my own bed. I said hello to the bunnies and they really do seem happy to hear my voice.

So, I am moving on and looking at this only in the rear view mirror now. It's all behind me (well close enough)!

Thanks for sticking with me everyone and for the prayers. Thank you so much for the prayers - they really pulled me through this one!

 # The Chair

Feb 21, 2014

If you've never experienced a miracle in your life or a clear and distinct sign from above, read on....

It was my first night home from the hospital and I was looking forward to sleeping in my own bed. My sister had changed and put clean sheets on while I was in the hospital and I was so looking forward to bedtime!

I came home from the hospital with a type of rash or pimples all up and down my back. With a drain on my left side and this on my back, that left me with one "good" side to sleep on. For this reason I did anticipate that I might not sleep too well so I took a Tylenol PM just for good measure. I managed to stay up until about 10:15pm watching the Olympic women's ice-skating finals though!

So I woke up around 12:15am to go to the bathroom. As I swung my legs out of bed my foot grazed something. I noticed a little black folding chair facing the bed. I keep this chair behind my bedroom door normally. A bit sleepy and a bit puzzled I wondered how it got there? I did the bathroom thing and came back into the bedroom and sat staring at the chair. I know I didn't put it there.... why would I have done that? I have absolutely no recollection of putting this chair there.

Then I remembered… the last thing I did as laid in bed on my "good" side was pray. Please God just help me get through this night. I need your help. The answer was obvious right then… that chair was put there to send me a message: "I am here and I am watching over you so you can rest."

I cried then and I cried again when I woke up and saw the chair again. I am leaving it right where it is as a reminder each night when I go to sleep. I am not alone. He is keeping vigil over me as I sleep. I have never had such a clear and distinct message in my life but I know this to be true.

I just wanted to share this with you all. I have always had strong faith and now it is even stronger. Calypso has absolutely no chance of getting the best of me…. not that he ever did, but he might as well wave the white flag. I KNOW how this story is going to end!

My friend Kelly sent me a video yesterday that really spoke directly to me. It's called "Overcomer" by Mandisa. I've downloaded this song to my iPod now. It's very inspirational.

Keeping the Faith….

And so on...

Another fun filled week of doctors' appointments and procedures. This really is a full time job!

I saw the plastic surgeon on Tuesday to have the drain removed. That was easy peasy. I go back next Tuesday to have the stitches removed. Things are healing very nicely and all signs of infection are gone.

Wednesday I had a follow up with the nurse practitioner. Again, easy peasy. We just went over all the details of my hospital vacation. It did NOT include a slide show.

Today I had my appointment with the ID (infectious Disease) doc. Very interesting visit... although I am giving myself IV antibiotics at home, I am not out of the woods yet. Seems this staph infection is a very nasty, sticky, slimy bacteria. It likes to attach itself to foreign objects in the body... especially metal devices, such as my beloved port. This bacteria can form a slime on the port and go into a dormant state for extended periods of time. It's more or less "hiding" from the antibiotics during this time. Once I am done with antibiotics and everything seems hunky dorey, the bacteria can "wake up" and attack the port. I'll add "stubborn and sneaky" to describe this bacteria. He's a little creeper!

So, in addition to the increased vocabulary I've gained this year, I can also add another skill set of giving myself IV antibiotics! I will continue these through next Tuesday, then we wait a week and see what happens. The other issue is that unlike the breast, if the port gets infected it will not present with those obvious symptoms of redness and swelling. More than likely I will get fever, chills and/or sweats. So I just have to be very mindful of how I am feeling in that critical week.

As long as there are no complications with the port, I will resume chemo on March 12th. That will be the last round of the combo A/C drug. I've been told that the Paclitaxel that I get weekly after this is usually much better tolerated. I figure since I've done so well with the A/C drug, this should be a snap!

I'm continuing to get out and walk every day and drink plenty of water & fluids. I think that has really helped to keep me strong and healthy (for the most part anyway). This staph thing is just a little bump in the road. We caught it early and we are on to it's sneaky, slimy ways so if it tries to come at me again, It's going to get a whoopin' just like Calypso! You all know by now that it takes a lot to keep me down. I am still in good spirits and surprising all the doctors by looking so healthy.

Thank you again for the support you all continue to give. I appreciate the thoughts and prayers, emails, phone calls, texts, etc. I certainly could not do this without all of you!

God Bless!

The Waiting Game

Mar 5, 2014

Today begins the waiting period to see if I will resume chemo next week. I finished the antibiotics yesterday and got the needle out of my port that had been there over two weeks. Nice to take a shower and be able to stand under the showerhead! It's those little things that make me happy!

So during this next week I have to be mindful that the little creeper bacteria may still be lingering and try to go after my port. Hopefully that won't happen. As long as I am in the clear next week we can get that last dose of AC over with.

I saw an orthopedic doc this week and got confirmation that my Sterno-Clavicular Joint is dislocated. I've been asking about this bump on my chest for weeks now... ever since the surgery to put my port in. When they put the port in they tried to do subclavian on both sides without success. A radiologist was brought in and he put it in the jugular vein. So, at some point when they were trying to do the subclavian they must have positioned my arm in such a way that the SC joint popped out of place. An X-ray was taken and said everything was normal. However, the Ortho-doc looked at the X-ray and took one look at me and said it's dislocated. There's nothing really to do other than not put too much strain on the right arm (it hurts a bit when I lift things or reach). It will eventually "fuse" together but the bump may never go away. Very strange - but I am lucky in that it popped outward (anterior) instead of inward (posterior). That could have caused problems with the trachea or other veins & arteries.

So, my list of doctors continues to grow. I got a call from an advocate with my health insurance and she asked me who was my doctor? That question will always make me laugh from now on as I rattle off the list!

Still, I am getting good care and no complaints. I'm just playing the waiting game now... taking my walks every day, which is usually followed by a nap. Fresh air and sunshine is helpful but also leaves me tired. At least the weather has been cooperating lately. Not that spring is here yet... after all, this is Colorado and we can have 70 degrees one day and a snow storm the next. Makes for an exciting week!

Not much else to tell then until next week. I appreciate all the well wishes and prayers. I continue to get cards in the mail too, which always puts a smile on my face. Thank you all for being there for me.

Until next time...

Now where was I????

Mar 11, 2014

Looks like the waiting game is over!

I have been feeling great since I stopped the antibiotics last week. I've seen the ID Doc and my plastic surgeon and both say all looks good. I continue to amaze them by how well I am doing and how good/healthy I look. I just had my labs done today and with the help of the online tool I have to keep me in touch with my medical records I can see that everything looks "normal" - even for me!

So, I will see the Oncologist tomorrow, then go for my last dose of the AC drug. Then in two weeks I will begin the Paclitaxel on a weekly basis for 12 weeks. That seems like a mighty long time but I'm sure I will do well and it will go by quickly. I am scheduled to go back to work later this month too, on a part time basis so that will help pass the time.

My mom is coming out in about a week along with my aunt. I am excited to see them both. Hopefully the weather will cooperate and we can get out and do some fun stuff before they leave and I go back to work. March in Colorado can bring quite a variety of weather. The past week was a mix of temps in the 30's with snow to blue skies and 70's. Just keep the flip-flops along side the winter boots and you'll be fine!

I haven't had much chance to wear the new wig but then I have at least 6 months to show it off, so there's no hurry. I like it but I have to admit the bandanas and scarves are just as easy to flip on the skull and head out the door. I just like to mix it up a bit.

Oh, I got a prescription for a prosthetic boob where my chest is flat from the removal of the expander. I guess I get a special bra and insert the device. The doc also said I could "stuff my bra" if I so desired. Glad to see he has a sense of humor! All looks good there too by the way. I have at least two more surgeries once chemo is done. One surgery to put an expander back in, then a second surgery to remove both of the temporary devices and put in the real deal!

That's the latest and greatest. I've been taking daily walks and hikes for the past week or so and feeling good and strong for tomorrow. Too bad for Calypso because the final tally after tomorrow will be:

Laura - Four for Four!

Calypso - big fat zero

Take that you slimy piece of worm ridden filth!

 # The results are in!

Mar 13, 2014

I have my fourth and final AC chemo treatment behind me now.

Final score (as predicted) is:
Laura - Four for Four!
Calypso – Big Fat ZERO

I got my labs done on Tuesday and all looked good. Then the visit with the Oncologist right before chemo and she also said all looked good. Off we went to the infusion lab where I got my recliner, warm blanket and lunch. Took a little snooze during the last part and all was good. Bobbie and Dawn were with me the entire time - always a comfort for me.

After Bobbie dropped me off I took a short walk to "blow the (chemo) stink off of me." Not to over do it but I did make a short trip to the store to pick up a few things. Then I took the night off and relaxed with a good book.

And that my friends, is how you kick some Calypso butt!

I will wait two weeks then start the weekly Taxol treatment. It's just one drug for 12 weeks so it should go a bit quicker. The pre-meds they give me are a bit different. No more steroid - yeah! But they will give me Benadryl, so I expect I will nap even more during treatment. I'll have to be sure to tell my drivers this so they can bring a book or magazine to entertain themselves!

And so the countdown begins - 12 more rounds. I really hope to get back to work soon. I am running out of things to do and though I am breezing though a lot of books, I really feel the need to be productive. We will get at least 2 doses of the Taxol on board so we know if I have any side effects, which are also different from the first combo cocktail. As long as I do well, which I fully expect, I can go back to work part-time. My life will start to feel a bit more "normal" then!

Stay tuned for more and thank you as always for joining me in my journey!

Hugs!

The Dirty Dozen

Mar 19, 2014

I have decided to break down the last twelve chemo treatments into what I call "The Dirty Dozen."

You know, there's Six of one/half a dozen of the other. A dime a dozen. Could be worse... could be a Bakers dozen, which is actually 13!

For some reason, I decided to make up a song about it. If you wondered about my "Chemo Brain" before, this will remove all doubt that I've lost it. Funny what being off work for several months will do to you and the ways you can find to amuse yourself!

Not as festive as the "Twelve days of Christmas" but here is how I foresee the remainder of the journey to play out in the "Twelve rounds of chemo." Sing along if you like (you know you will)!

On the 1st round of chemo, my doctor said to me:
The Benadryl will help you sleep it off.
On the 2nd round of chemo, my doctor said to me:
Pepcid for your tummy and
On the 3rd round of chemo, my doctor said to me:
Have a nice warm blanket
On the 4th round of chemo my doctor said to me:
Don't forget to hydrate

On the 5th round of chemo my doctor said to me:
Almost halfway there!
On the 6th round of chemo my doctor said to me:
6 down 6 to go, you're
On the 7th round of chemo my doctor said to me:
Looking really good now
On the 8th round of chemo my doctor said to me:
You're an overcomer!
On the 9th round of chemo my doctor said to me:
Have a piece of chocolate
On the 10th round of chemo my doctor said to me:
Getting really close now
On the 11th round of chemo my doctor said to me:
Can you see the finish?
And…
On the 12th round of chemo my doctor said to me:
Now it's time to party!
Can you see the finish?
Getting really close now
Have piece of chocolate
You're an overcomer!
Looking really good now
6 down 6 to go, you're
Almost halfway there!
Don't forget to hydrate
Have a nice warm blanket
Pepcid for your tummy and
The Benadryl will help you sleep it off.

The Benadryl will help you sleep it off!

Mar 26, 2014

Today was the first day of the Paclitaxel (Taxol for short). One down, eleven to go. They gave me the Benadryl after giving me Dexamethazone (steroid) and Pepcid for the tummy. The Benadryl did make me sleep/groggy but it also gave me restless legs/ankles so I couldn't sleep. They decided next time they will reduce the dose by half since I did so well. No other side effects or reactions - yeah me!

My mom and Aunt Mary came for a visit this past weekend. We had a lot of fun and laughs, and shopped 'til we dropped. I'm glad mom got to see for herself how well I am doing and that Eva, Bobbie and Dawn are taking excellent care of me. Other than the baldhead and that I tire more easily I don't think there is much different about me, so rest assured mom - I'm doing just fine!

I've been having a little fun with the wigs lately. I have people doing double takes when they see me and that goes for both wigs, not just the red head! I've decided the red head is my evil twin, so anytime I do something bad, I will blame it on her... Lulu. She is shameless. With the weather warming up, it's actually easier to just tie a bandana on my head so I'll be saving the wigs for special occasions (and for shaking things up).

Glad to have the first of these treatments done now. It's still early but I think I am going to do just fine. This drug is supposed to be much easier tolerated than the first two and I did very well with that so I don't anticipate any problems. I am off next week then going back to work part-time the following week. Looking forward to some structure in my days again!

That's it for now. Thanks for following and for the support. Here's a photo so you will remember to look out for Lulu... she's a trouble-maker that one!

In loving memory
of Jim DiNapoli

Mar 29, 2014

My dear friend Jim lost his battle with pancreatic cancer today. Jim was by far the most amazing and complex person I've ever met. He was a physician with many passions. His musical talent extended to piano, guitar and bass. All who knew him know of his love for rock climbing - a passion he carried for over 35 years and taught many the sport. As an avid mountaineer, he climbed every 14er in Colorado and then went back to do them all in winter.

He made it to 44 of them and had planned to finish up this winter. He was an amazing photographer and an accomplished bicycle racer and competitor as well. Seems he was happiest when he was on top of the world or moving at the speed of light.

He was diagnosed with cancer about a week after I got my breast cancer diagnosis last year. For whatever reason we were linked together through our separate battles. He was blessed to have time to spend with his friends before his passing. He is no longer in pain and left this earth knowing he is loved.

Hiking Limbaugh Canyon – July 2013

Pepcid for my tummy

Apr 3, 2014

Time for another update... yesterday was Taxol #2 and all went well. They were able to reduce the Benadryl to 25mg - half what they gave me last week. It helped quite a bit with the UNhappy feet so I was able to sleep a bit. Still need to tweak or add something to eliminate this all together. I could have used a longer nap! Next we will see about reducing the IV steroids a bit. At least I don't have to take the pills for the 3 days after any longer. Those make me moody and emotional.

Speaking of moody and emotional... it was a long, quiet weekend for me. I was really sad about losing Jim. Even though I knew it was coming soon I guess you are just never prepared for it. He was one heckuva guy and he changed my life. He will continue to change it too as I strive to become a better person. His good friend and caretaker Mike has been there for me since. He and I went for a hike at Red Rock Canyon open space on Tuesday and sat up high on a rock and had a really long, good talk. Jim was so blessed to have such a good friend and because of the events over the past few months, Mike is my good friend as well. Another blessing in my life!

Speaking of blessings.... Dawn and Bobbie are hosting an open house fundraiser for me this Sunday. If you are in Colorado, you should check it out. There will be food and LOTS of very nice jewelry (Park Lane) for sale at about 75% off the regular price. I've already called "dibs" on a few pieces... and I'm not even a big jewelry wearer.

I have two more days (plus the weekend) before heading back to work. I will start back part time, 4 hours a day so I can get labs done on Tuesday and chemo on Wednesday. I also have time for naps if needed. I am so fortunate to have a job with benefits to allow me time to heal completely. I know people who have gone through this under much worse circumstances... working full time, kids to take care of, no support, etc. As I've said before - for someone who was diagnosed with cancer, I feel truly blessed.

It can't be said enough... thank you all for coming along on the journey with me. Just knowing you are there with me makes it a much easier path to take!

 # Gratitude

Apr 7, 2014

I am so blessed to have such amazing people in my life.

It was a good weekend. Friday I went for a 5-mile hike with a friend. It was mostly flat, but still!!! That is the most I have done in awhile!

Saturday I was signed up for an 18-mile bike ride. I really wanted to dust off the bike and see how I would do. I figured I could always stop and go back at any point if I got too tired. We ended up doing just under 12 miles with a lunch stop in the middle, so it worked out well and I did just fine. My body was a bit tired and sore but no more than any other time I work out.

On Sunday, my dear friends Bobbie and Dawn held an open house fundraiser for me. Dawn sold her inventory of Park Lane jewelry at huge discounts with 50% of the proceeds to help with my medical bills. Bobbie cooked and served scrumptious food and opened her home to the event. It was a great success and so much fun. I think talking and socializing with everyone was every bit as tiring as that bike ride! But what a nice way to spend the day and what amazing friends I have to continue to do so much for me. I am so very blessed.

I sometimes feel guilty and a little undeserving of such support when I know there are others that are struggling more than I am. What have

I done to deserve all this? I am reminded of that song from the Sound of Music.... "somewhere in my youth or childhood, I must have done something good." My sisters would probably disagree with that though... haha!

All I can do is know that when this is over and I am put in a position to help others (and I know I will be) I will do anything and everything I can to pay it forward. I just have a feeling that before this year is over my life is going to be taking a new direction. This has all happened for a reason.... so stay tuned!

I went back to work today. I am only working 4 hours a day right now so I can have time for lab work, doctor appointments and of course chemo on Wednesday... not to mention naps. It was nice to be back and my co-workers all sent words of encouragement. I'm sure it will all come back to me quickly but after 5 months of not working, I was beginning to wonder! I have a kazillion emails to sort through as you can imagine too. Still, I am not complaining. I am fortunate to have a great job with great benefits.

Labs and doctor tomorrow and chemo on Wednesday.... and of course it's supposed to be in the 70's on Wednesday. Hopefully I can take a short walk after and once again "blow the chemo stink off me."

Feeling very blessed and grateful today. Life is good!

Have a nice warm blanket

Apr 9, 2014

Taxol #3 is in the history books. Coincidentally I needed that nice warm blanket today. I was over in the west wing corner and it was cold there! I got two blankets actually!

I think we have tweaked the pre-meds enough now that I am more comfortable and the UNhappy feet are doing much better. Unfortunately part of that equation was adding an Ativan pill for anxiety. I'm not a believer of giving a pill to counteract another pill but in this case I will comply. It's only once a week for 9 more weeks and it allows me to sleep! Bobbie was my ride today, so once they started the sleepy-time drugs I told her to go home for a bit since I was going to sleep for the next 1.5 hours. Fortunately she lives just 5 blocks away!

The jewelry fundraiser on Sunday went very well. It was so very kind of Dawn to donate part of the proceeds from her own inventory. I have amazing friends. The Pay Forward fund-raiser had helped me to catch up on the 2013 bills and most of the 2014 bills, so between the two events all my medical bills are paid up for now! Yeah... much less stress in my life!

I want to send out a heartfelt thank you to all who contributed. It is never an easy thing to ask for help and I was so hesitant to do so. My friends assured me that it was okay to ask because people wanted to help. That became very apparent once I agreed. Ya'all really made a huge difference in my life and I will never forget it.

I am hoping to recuperate (physically and financially) enough by the fall to enjoy some group trips and outdoor fun. We have a camp out scheduled for August and Dawn has a timeshare in Durango for a long weekend in July. A few friends and I had planned a week of backpacking in Italy this year. We couldn't do it in May as planned but I am hoping that maybe somehow I can make it happen in the fall. Doesn't seem likely but then there's always next year! If I am physically able, I'd like to get in another 14er or two this fall. Those last two are more of a "wait and see." At least it's nice to make plans and have something to look forward to after this long journey. I just know I will be ready to celebrate!!!

So far, so good at work this week. I am working 8am-noon Monday through Friday for a few weeks. Then I'll be back full-time and just take a little time off for the lab work and chemo. I only have to see the doctor every 2-3 weeks now so that's one less appointment. I pray that things continue to go as well as they have. I am so very blessed to continue to enjoy good health through this journey.

Well, time to get my own nice, warm blanket and head to bed. Long day!

Nighty night - sleep tight and don't let those bed bugs bite!

Don't forget to hydrate!

Apr 16, 2014

Hydration was a good one for today as it rained most of the time I was in the infusion lab. Our grounds need the hydration as much as I do!

I am officially halfway done with all chemo (includes the AC portion). Eight down, eight to go. At least the "to go" number will be going down each week now and I really need to see that! It feels like these last eight treatments are going in slow motion. Where's that remote? I need to Fast Forward!

Okay, so my patience is being tested I know. I also know that "patience is a virtue." I believe impatience is a virtue as well, right? Still I am glad the numbers are going down and I'm feeling good and doing well. The nurses are all kind of wondering what I am doing that keeps me from having any side effects whatsoever. Other than a little fatigue, I am perfectly normal! My sister will be LOL at that last remark.

My dear friend Mike took me to chemo today and everything was absolutely hunky dorey. We decided to forget eating a healthy diet... toxic chemicals seem to do it for me! I question it a bit myself but I'm certainly not going to complain. It's a gift and I will accept it with much gratitude. I still think I may end up with super powers before it's all over!

It was a fun day today. Mike had accompanied Jim to all of his chemo treatments and they were nothing like mine. For one, we were offered Tiramisu when we got there. I guess a patient brought it in so they were sharing. We talked and laughed with the nurses and aides and he couldn't believe chemo could be so much fun.

The Benadryl & Ativan are still battling each other somewhere in my lower extremities. I do manage to snooze a bit but the leg thing is annoying. The nurse is going to check with the doctor to see if I really need the Benadryl since I am not having any reactions or side effects. Maybe next week we will get the "secret formula" perfected!

I have fuzz growing on my head. I shaved the top clean once because the fuzz was itchy. Now it's growing back... about 1/4-1/2 inch. I never did lose it all… I still had some on the sides so I guess you could picture me sporting the "old guy" look. I'm not sure if it will continue to grow but I hope so. I don't wear the wigs a lot because they are hot and kinda itchy. Now that I have fuzz again it will itch even more. I miss having hair. Fuzz just isn't the same thing.

Well, that was my exciting day of chemo. Work has been okay - just mornings for now so I can fit in appointments. I may have to continue until chemo is done but we'll see how it goes.

It just keeps getting more and more exciting, doesn't it? I hope you aren't bored with this yet. I am, so I suspect some of you are. Still, we keep taking that step.... just one step at a time!

 # Almost halfway there!

Apr 23, 2014

So technically I was halfway done with **all** chemo last week. With the Paclitaxel I am on #5 with 7 remaining so next week will be 6/6. Overall, I've had 9 rounds of chemo so I am just happy to be on the count DOWN side of things!

I sometimes get that same feeling I had when we took long car rides as children and often think "Are we there yet?" This seems like it's just taking so long to finish but the weeks are counting down and the weather is heating up. I should be done by mid-June then I can put my toxic-diet behind me and go back to my "normal" life!

Everything went really well today. My friend Greg was my ride and kept me entertained with stories and a friendly game of Scrabble (aka. the non-scoring type game). We did a game night at Fargo's last night and I laughed so much my face hurt, so I didn't mind the quiet pace of our game! He hadn't played in years and kept trying to use Spanish words so I had to keep an eye on him.

The best news is that I did not have to get the Benadryl, therefore no Ativan either! I was still a little tired and tried to take a quick nap but no go. I didn't mind at all. I was just happy to have fewer drugs in my system.

The skies were looking quite stormy when I got home so I dared not get out to walk. Last time I tempted the Colorado skies I ended up a soaked, drowning rat!

I had a visitor early this evening. My neighbors' daughter Kayla (11 years old) came over and said she heard that I had Calypso. I told her yes, I did and she handed me a hand made card and a rubber band bracelet that she made. That was just so sweet! I gave her a hug and thanked her. These are the same neighbors that helped to shovel my driveway when it snowed. I am so blessed to have such considerate neighbors!

My other neighbor that lives in the other half of the duplex gave me the name of a woman she works with and has a lunch get together once a month for survivors. I joined them for lunch last week at their church and they gave me a prayer shawl. Since I am still working part time I will try to join them for another one or two before I get back to that 40-hour-week stuff!

I hope this finds everyone feeling healthy and strong like myself! I would not feel this way if not for your support and prayers! As always, a heartfelt thank-you to you all!

Six down, Six to go now!

Apr 30, 2014

Sometimes I think of the six remaining and think "Wow - that's not many at all!" Other days, I think "I STILL have six more to go? Really???"

So, today I read this little ditty and it helped:

You need to be content with small steps. That's all life is. Small steps that you take every day so when you look back down the road it all adds up and you know you covered some distance. It may take time to accept this but it's true. You need to have patience.

So today was one more small step and I only have six more small steps to take. In the grand scheme of things, that is really not much at all. I am very glad that we are doing these weekly now instead of every other week. That helps it to go by a little quicker too!

My escort for today's chemo was my friend Matt. We have both been busy this past week so this gave us time to catch up a bit. It can be a little boring but it can also be quite fascinating with all the technology they use. Thank you Matt for the ride and for spending time with me today.

When I saw the Nurse Practitioner yesterday she checked with the Pharmacist and we cut the steroids in half now! Only 4mg! We may even be able to discontinue if I continue to do well. I sure hope so because I have put on 10 pounds and always leave there feeling like I swallowed a water balloon! UGH!

So that's really all the news for now. Today was "easy-peasy-lemon-squeezy!"

 # Looking really good now!

May 7, 2014

It always amazes me how much difference a day can make. A week makes quite a difference sometimes too!

I found myself saying for the last two treatments "I have 6 (or 7) left - dang that's a lot." For some reason this week I was thinking "I ONLY have 5 left - wow!" It's like I can actually see the light at the end of the tunnel and for some reason I am feeling better about this. Looking forward to the end of this toxic diet I've been on. And you thought eating celery and rabbit food was a challenging diet!

So we have reduced the steroids to 4mg for two weeks now and I've asked for next week that we discontinue them all together. Hopefully that will happen because I always feel like I swallowed a water balloon when I walk out of there. Still, I guess if that's my only trouble I am doing okay, right?

We (friends of Jim) had a "Celebration of Life" on Saturday and it couldn't have been a more perfect day. We did rock climbing in the Gardens then had a memorial service in the afternoon at the Gardens followed by an evening gathering. I was pleasantly surprised at how many people came to each event. Some attended all day and oh, the stories that were told! That man really touched a whole lotta lives!

I had a really hard time for a few days after that. It just made things feel so "final." I cried a lot over those few days and I prayed a lot too. I asked for help to be at peace with all that has happened and all that I felt and to move on. This morning I woke up feeling just that... peaceful.

Sure, I have questions that will never be answered and there are things that transpired over Jim's final weeks that I won't understand. These are the things that have kept me awake at night for weeks. I know that I cannot change any of that and I can't get him back. It's time to "let it go" and to move on and I am okay with that now. He will always be in my heart and we will meet again one day.

So a week or a day, even a minute can certainly make quite a difference. You just never know what or how things can just turn around and be okay.

Now if I can just get my career and future to feel "okay!" The time is coming I know... patience.

 # You're an Overcomer!

May 14, 2014

I certainly feel like I am finally "overcoming" this part of my journey! After today it's "Four to go, then no mo!"

I hitched a ride from my friend Amy K today. She was kind enough to pick me up and spend some good quality time hanging out at the infusion center. I really know how to show my friends a good time!

Everything went very well. I still had to take the steroids but just the 4mg IV dose so not the worst thing. I guess they feel like I've reached my limit in discontinuing or asking to NOT get so many drugs. So pre-meds or "appetizers" as I call them are still Pepcid and Dexamethazone (steroids). The main course remains the same - Paclitaxel or Taxol for short. I am tolerating it well but my blood work has been going down ever so slightly. Hopefully it won't go down much more so I can finish this up on schedule and not have to delay.

I was talking to another chemo patient (Teresa) with a similar situation to mine. The main difference with us is that she did the Paclitaxel first then the A/C combo. So hers was just the opposite from my treatment. I saw her several weeks ago before she started the A/C and she was concerned because she heard bad stories. Mine was the first positive experience she heard so that made her feel better and after seeing her today and talking to her, she is doing about as well as I did! We swapped stories and laughed a lot. She is funny and has a good attitude like me. We figured out that we are going to finish on the same day if all stays on schedule - June 11ᵗʰ. I think things may get a little crazy at the infusion center that day!

Other than putting on about 10 pounds in the past few weeks I am not having any problems. I am blaming the steroids for the most part... at least that's my story and I'm sticking to it. I just don't look like a chemo patient and I am starting to suspect that chemo gives you super powers. I feel bad when other patients tell me how they are suffering from the drugs and treatments, but there isn't much I can say since my experience is totally different. I continue to be grateful for maintaining good health during my toxic diet plan. With the end so close, I pray that continues.

Since I have been feeling so good I have been scheduling events for the Outdoor Club. I did a six mile hike on Saturday, which was just lovely and felt so good to get out again! I have to admit it kinda kicked my butt though. I came home and cleaned up and took a nap and didn't do much else the rest of the day. Still... it felt really good to get out. Since we had a snow day on Sunday I was grateful for the beautiful weather on Saturday.

All in all it was a good day today. Thank you Amy for taking time to help me out. I enjoyed the company and the game of Scrabble! You are still the "Heads Up" queen... I rule Scrabble.

And my continued thanks and gratitude to all who have taken this journey with me and sent prayers and supported me. Each step gets us closer and closer and I know I will look back soon to discover that I've conquered quite the mountain!

Zip lining on May 17th. Don't all chemo patients do this?

Have a piece of chocolate!

May 21, 2014

Because that is my answer to everything! At first I thought Chocolate might be the cure for Calypso!

Alas, I have been trying to cut down on the chocolate because the steroids are making me put on weight and I feel really pudgy right now. So I'll settle for some non-fat sherbet!

My friend Pam took me to chemo today. The nurses and others at the lab love meeting all the people that I bring in. I think it's interesting for those that come too. I have all of my rides lined up for the remaining treatments but anyone can stop by to visit if you like. I have only THREE MORE and they are all Wednesday afternoons. I'm there from about 2:30pm until 5:30pm so let me know if you want to stop by and I'll get you the details.

Pam got a nice education today. She must have asked me at least a dozen times "Do you feel that going into your body?" and a slight variation…"Do you feel anything from that?" I just laughed and so did the nurse. I am certainly not a typical chemo patient. I think she envisioned me laid out on a bed with tubes coming out of my body and not able to move. We played a few games of Sorry, which was a blast. I hadn't played in so long. She let me win and I didn't even have to play the C-Card!

So now we are down to the final three! It's 3-2-1 and done!

I am getting very antsy too! At least it's every week and not every other week as with the first two drugs. Once chemo is done I can see the plastic surgeon and see if I get the booby prize for sticking with it!

I appreciate all of you who follow me in this journey. I do see and get notifications when I get any "action" on the website so please know that I am aware of those who have followed me from the start and those who just pop in from time to time to see if anything interesting is happening (or if there is any boob talk). Please know how much it means to me that you've come this far with me. I hope you will see me through to the finish... and party with me afterwards!

Getting really close now!

May 28, 2014

And then there were two....

I can't believe I only have two left! It was harder when I thought about having 4 or 5 left but now with ONLY two I am really getting excited. It's almost time to party! I think the party date is going to be June 20, so keep that date open for those who live in the Springs.

Bobbie was my ride today. I managed to stay awake the entire time even though I was tired from tossing and turning the night before. We have both been busy so it was nice to have a couple hours to catch up. I got out for a short walk before hand as well since the weather was gorgeous.

I did a hike on Saturday that was so pretty. The flowers and cactus were starting to bloom and we had a creek (aka river at the time) to follow the entire way. It was a little scary crossing the first two times going in – the water was rushing up over my knees! Coming back the next two times weren't so bad. I didn't realize until later that I had my cell phone, camera, wallet and car keys in my waist pack. A fall in the water would not have been good! Nobody said us hikers always use common sense (or Ziplock bags). The hike was about 6 miles with a lot of ups & downs, like a roller-coaster... however, I did not raise my hands in the air and go running down the hill screaming (though that would not have surprised anyone if I had done it).

The hike did leave me pretty drained. I didn't do much the rest of the day but I did get out more over the weekend. I went to Territory Days in Old Colorado City on Sunday with Dawn. Bad weather scared us off so we didn't stay long.

Other than that, it's been a rather uneventful week. I am trying not to overdo things so I can get this chemo party wrapped up and move on to more fun things, like reconstruction. This is certainly going to be a year to remember, that's for sure.

Oh, check out the photo I just added... my hair is already growing back! At least I'll have a short, cool cut for summer - but there is definitely hair there!

So until next time, I'll be singing "and a one and a two, and a one and a two, and a one and a two..."

Gettin' "fuzzy"

Can you see the finish?

Jun 4, 2014

I sure can! It's like at the end of a really long hike and we are coming down the trail with the parking lot in view and I look forward to my favorite part.... taking off the shoes and putting on flip flops!

Now with the chemo, I think my favorite part will be getting the port yanked out.

So, just ONE more... Uno. Ein. Jeden. Un. Bir. Een. Otu. Unum. Um. Moja. Ett. ONE!

Try and figure out the languages if you like... answers are at the bottom! Consider this your education for the day. I could have added more but these were the words that amused me at the moment.

I went to get my labs done yesterday as I do every week before chemo. I did have to add one last culture labs as well for the 3-month check up on the infection that I had in February. Remember that sticky, slimy little bugger? Remember I was told it could "hang out" around the port for months? Well, this should be the last check to make sure that pesky little stinker is really gone for good.

Anyway... the one time that they need to draw blood from my port without flushing first (not talking about the bathroom here) they couldn't get blood return. They did end up flushing, which is pushing saline through to clear the line. Still, no blood return. I can't get cultures or blood or chemo unless they get that blood return... big UH OH!

So, they had me lean forward and touch my toes. They had me cough. Then they laid me flat and I laid on my left side, then my right side. Then I walked up and down the hall flapping my arms and I did jumping jacks. I swear I expected someone from Candid Camera to pop out at any moment! All of this was to hopefully "pop" loose whatever was clogging the port. We had almost given up when the head nurse came over and gave the syringe a quick tug and got the blood return. Talk about a magic touch!

We had a good laugh over it and everything came back looking good so I had my second to last infusion today! Coincidentally I had the same nurse today that drew my labs yesterday, so we had a more laughs about the whole ordeal.

My friend Laura was my ride today. It was so good to catch up with her. We took a couple games to keep us busy and she brought magazines. We didn't get to any of them really... we just yacked away those 4 hours! She is hosting my "No-Mo-Chemo" party on June 20th so if you are in the Springs, stay tuned for details. If you are not in the Springs and want to come, let me know!

It's a rather bittersweet thing, this end of chemo. I can't say enough good things about the nurses and admin staff in the Oncology department at Memorial. I was pretty easy for them (I think) but I've seen them handle quite a bit while there. I told several of them "You are the most wonderful people that I never want to see again!"

So what's next on the agenda? Well, I've got an appointment with the plastic surgeon on the 17th to take measurements and talk surgery to put the left expander (temporary implant) back in. I also called the Oncology Surgeon about removing the port. My last chemo is June 11 so if I had my way, it would come out on June 12. Patience is not always a virtue for me. Well, that's not an option I am told. We need to wait a few weeks and make sure my blood counts come back up to normal so it will most likely come out when we do the expander surgery. Once the expander is in for a month or so I get one last surgery to put in the "real deal"... the permanent implants. I'm sure there will be follow up appointments and such but I hope to be done with the surgeries before the end of August and definitely by Labor Day. I'd like to enjoy the last quarter of 2014 in a more "normal" fashion if possible.

Can you believe I've been doing this chemo thing for a almost 6 months? Sixteen infusions! I must have some pretty amazing super powers by now! I've decided that once I am done with having chemicals infused into my system I am going to proceed with flushing them all out the old fashioned way.... with lots of alcohol! Ha-ha! Just kidding - I am simply looking forward to having a nice glass of wine now and then or a cold beer after a long, hot day of hiking! I wasn't restricted from alcohol during chemo and I did indulge a few times but since I was doing so well I didn't want to push my luck, so I abstained (for the most part).

Well, The finish line is in sight and I'm really psyched about next week. I believe my BED team will be accompanying me but anyone in the Springs is welcome to stop by and visit. I'll be at the infusion lab from about 2:00pm until 5:30-6:00pm. Call or text if you aren't sure or have questions. I'd love to go out in party mode!

Thank you again everyone who has supported me with your visits, phone calls, rides to chemo, words of encouragement, donations to the fund raiser, sending prayers, etc. You have all been my rock stars and I could not have done this without you. A very profound thank-you from the bottom of my heart.

Now let's rock this thing next week!

Answers to the ONE quiz:

Italian, German, Czech, French, Turkish, Dutch, Igbo, Latin, Portuguese, Swahili, Swedish, English.

# Now it's time to party!

Jun 11, 2014

No Mo Chemo! I had my last treatment today - Yippee! It was uneventful as far as treatments go which is a good thing. I was actually looking forward to this day and it was made even better by the good company of friends and family.

My sister Eva was my ride. Bobbie met us there then Matt and Mike came by and visited as well. It was a great way to pass the time. We closed the place down around 5:15pm so decided to go to dinner and tried a new place called Lucha Cantina. I think everyone liked it. My taste buds have been a little off lately so mine was just "okay." Besides, it wasn't the food that made the night fun - it was the company. Terry and Paul joined Bobbie, Eva, Matt and I so it was a nice celebration with lots of laughs.

There was thunder and rain as we headed to the hospital today. I was thinking "I'm gonna go out with a big bang!" We've been getting quite a bit of moisture lately, which is good - keeps the fire danger down and everything green. Can't wait to get out and do more hiking and get my energy levels back to my kind of normal!

So, what's next? I have decided not to do radiation and I'm 100% good with that decision. I met with my Oncology Doctor yesterday and we discussed the hormone blocking agents and the possible side effects. I tell you, when they can create a medication that doesn't have any side effects that are worse than what's being treated - now THAT will be progress in the medical world! Still, the hormone blocking pill is shown to help reduce the recurrence of cancer even more so than chemo alone so it's a necessary evil. I just need to decide which one to go with and of course see if I do okay with it and if not, we try a different one. It's hit or miss I guess!

I meet with the Plastic Surgeon next week and will ask him to remove the port when he does his thing. My Oncology Surgeon wanted to take it out in the office but I am not comfortable with that. She had trouble putting it in, so I feel better having it removed in a surgical setting and this way I will be asleep while they do it - even better.

So, that's what is on the agenda for me. I will still have some follow up appointments and frequent checks. I will most likely need an injection to help protect my bones and a bone density test. There is still a lot of information coming at me. Sure makes chemo seem easy.... all I had to do was go sit in a chair and make the nurses laugh for a couple hours!

So happy today is over and chemo treatments are in the rear view mirror now. I will happily look to the future now and see what it brings for me next! One thing I know for sure after all of this... I can handle whatever comes my way... with a little help from my friends of course!

Thank you all for the good wishes today and for those who kept me company. Once again - you are the foundation of my support system and my gratitude runs deep.

 # No Mo Chemo

Jun 20, 2014

It's been a little over a week since my last chemo. Feels good NOT to have that stuff pumped into my body. Funny thing is that this past week I have been feeling the effects more than I did all during treatment. I guess it finally caught up with me in the end!

Other than being more tired than usual I think I am finally feeling (my version of) normal again! I've been hiking and biking as much as I can and I can only hope that my energy levels will continue to improve.

Laura and Craig are throwing a "No-Mo-Chemo" party for me tonight. I may have no-mo-chemo, but I will definitely be having an adult beverage of some kind to celebrate!

I can't even put into words (which is unusual for me) how much it means to me to have friends and family take this journey with me. I have seen a lot of people at the infusion center who are alone and have heard stories that make my journey pale in comparison. So I hope you all know how truly grateful I am that you take the time to ask how I am doing or text, call, email me to check in. Those who have been my rides to chemo, I hope you know how much I appreciate that. These may seem like small gestures to you, but to me they all add up to a whole lotta love from good friends and family!

Last but certainly not least – to my BED team. Kelly this includes you. You ladies rock! I couldn't have asked for a better support system and the fact is I didn't even have to ask you. You all just stepped in and did what needed to be done. I don't even know how to begin to thank you all. As I used to tell my sister Eva when we were growing up and I wanted a favor or something from her... "If you ever break your leg and need me, I'll be there for you!" Only difference now is I mean it!

I still have some follow up - two surgeries and doctor visits and such. For the most part I think my life will be getting back to normal... at least for my physical well-being. I am still contemplating a career change. This journey and my journey with Jim's passing have taught me a lot this year. Life is too short to do anything less than what you love. I am processing ideas and putting my trust in God that He has a plan for me. The answers will come... I just need to be aware and pay attention (otherwise the answers may need to smack me upside the head)!

Until next time...

Yes, I'm still out here!

July 7, 2014

Yes, all the chemo excitement has been done for three weeks now but I have surgery to look forward to next. My energy levels have come up since I stopped the toxic diet and I've been hiking a bit. Oh, and I biked down Pikes Peak this past weekend with my niece Jen but that was only 19.8 miles.

I just finished downloading my journal entries and hope to put it into book format and have it published. Do you think anyone would buy it? I'm just a crazy woman who had a Calypso experience and a short chemo diet. I guess I shouldn't call it a chemo diet though since I actually put on about 15 pounds during round two!

I'm looking forward to getting this next phase done, even though it's going to be drawn out for a few weeks and then a month or so to make sure these ta-ta's are going to work for me before the permanent ones are put into place. Hopefully there will still be enough summer left so I can wear some skimpy sun dresses and show these perky girls off a bit!

I followed up with the Oncologist and I have decided not to do radiation. The risks seem to outweigh the benefits for me at this point and could really complicate the upcoming surgeries so that's my decision and I'm 100% certain it's the right one for me. I started the hormone-blocking pill called Letrozole. I'll be on that for at least 5 years - probably more. The most common side effects are hot flashes and joint pain. Really? Heck, I already have those so I guess we'll give it a whirl!

I'll keep you all "abreast" of the surgery outcome. I am told once the initial mastectomy is done, this is considered an "easy" procedure. I just love a male doctor telling me that cutting on my boobs is easy.

Stay tuned for the next installment in about a week!

 # A day of Déjà vu anyone?

Jul 16, 2014

Another successful surgery is in the rear view mirror now. That leaves just one more before I am free and it's time to bid farewell to all my doctor and nurse friends and get back to my hiking and outdoor friends!

Things were rather uneventful today. Pretty much the same as the last couple surgeries with the exception of not having my BED team. It was just "E" and me. Bobbie already had vacation plans when the appointment was made so I had E&D left. Then Dawn went and got sick this week and couldn't talk! That left Eva and I knew she wouldn't let me down. I missed my other girls though. I had my friend Mike on "standby" just in case though!

We got checked in and then the doc came in and drew all over my chest and put the word "YES" near my port so that wouldn't get overlooked. I was almost as anxious for that to come out as I was to get the reconstruction zone back in play. Once again the nurses and all staff were just wonderful. They make it all so easy to go through - almost to the point that I don't mind having the procedure.... Almost!

I was in and out in about an hour and Eva was back with me in recovery about 30 minutes after that. We hung out for a bit, I got more drugs and headed home around 4pm or so. I had myself a little Vicodin coma like sleep when I got home so Eva stuck around to make sure I woke up!

I'm finally feeling more alert this evening. Glad to have this behind me. I go back to see the doc next Wednesday to have the drain removed. Yes, I have a drain again! Then the following week we get to start to "fill-er-up" again. Déjà vu – fun times indeed.

I'll be taking it easy while I have the drain in, which is the secret to getting it to drain less. Less activity = less output... unfortunately because I am ready to hit the trails again soon!

That is the latest and greatest for me. Hope to just kick back and visit some friends while I am laid up, so if you're in the Springs, do stop by and visit!

Complication?

July 17, 2014

About 8pm tonight I was cleaning up my torso from the surgical procedure. I had that betadyne stain from my neck to my nether regions.

I discovered something very disturbing... the port was obviously removed but the line that went from the port to my jugular vein appeared to still be in place! I can see and feel it just as it was prior to surgery. Does that mean that the incision was made, the port was removed and the catheter was tied off and left right where it is?

I don't know what to do. Obviously I will call the doctors office in the morning first thing but I wonder if this was intentional? Why would they do that? I cannot live with a catheter in my jugular vein for the rest of my life. This thing has had me worried since day one and the thought of it being in there forever just tied off to nowhere scares me even more. It's almost 2:00am and I haven't slept yet!

I may be over reacting a bit here but this whole port placement has been an issue since that first surgery on January 7. The surgeon had trouble trying to insert it sub-clavian on both the right and left sides so she had the radiologist put it in the right internal-jugular vein. At least it was in so I thought it was okay. A few days later I noticed that I had a large lump where the clavical and sternum meet, known as the sterno-clavicular joint (SCJ). I pointed it out to the Nurse Practitioner who thought it might be swelling. A few weeks later it was still protruding so I pointed it out again and an x-ray was done. The x-ray showed normal. I was not satisfied with that answer so I asked my late friend Jim, who was a doctor and he said it looks like the SCJ is dislocated.

I made an appointment and had an orthopedic doc look at it, and he immediately confirmed that it was dislocated. Said he sees it all the time but it's usually some pretty forceful trauma that causes it. There's nothing to be done since wiring it or putting pins in could cause more problems. Time would heal it but it may always protrude. I should gain most of my strength back also.

I could live with that but nobody would claim responsibility for it. I am certain that it happened during the port placement. So now, as if this thing hasn't been problematic enough I will still need to have the catheter pulled out? Do I let the same surgeon who pulled the port out do it or the one who couldn't get it in the first time? The main reason I asked to have it done when they put the temporary filler back in is so I could be in a surgical setting and be monitored for a while afterwards. I am overly concerned about this and need some advice. This just seems unacceptable. Did they think I wouldn't notice or is this standard practice?

Geeze, I need some sleep. Guess I'll take a pill.

Update:
After a call to the after hours line and speaking with the RN that was assisting the doc, I've been reassured that the catheter was removed with the port. Next question: so what am I feeling there? Answer: could be a spasm or scar tissue.

I'm not entirely satisfied with this answer but maybe enough so I can sleep a bit since the sun will be up in two hours. I will try to confirm and talk with the doctor tomorrow since he did not talk to either my sister or myself after the surgery today. We saw him beforehand of course. He was supposed to come out and tell Eva how the procedure went but then he got pulled into another surgery while I was in recovery so I didn't get to see him afterwards at all.

Addendum:

Note to self... Don't call, text or write stuff when you are sleep deprived and on drugs. It's the equivalent of drunk dialing your ex. I just kinda rambled on and on, didn't I? Feeling a bit better today but plan to lay low and let my body heal.

# Interesting stuff

July 18, 2014

Okay, now that I am off pain meds I am thinking a little clearer. I think part of my panic attack the other night was due to those meds. I still think something is rather peculiar where the port and catheter were but I'll get answers to that when I see the surgeon on Wednesday.

I had a dentist appointment on Monday last week prior to surgery. I had to get clearance to get the Zometa injection since it can cause problems in the jawbone. The funny thing about this visit is that the hygienist spent very little time cleaning. Normally I have a lot of plaque... even though I brush, floss, use mouthwash - it's just a genetic thing. Well, apparently chemo kills plaque too. That's my guess. I can't believe how quick and easy that visit went! We had a good laugh over it anyway!

Another peculiar thing is that my eyebrows and eyelashes are falling out... almost completely. That doesn't make sense since the hair on my head is getting longer and fuller every day. I know the chemo changes your body chemistry but I sure hope I get those back... not that I wear makeup a lot but I kinda like having eyebrows and eyelashes! Now the hair on my legs - I don't really care if that comes back. Am I being too selective here?

Other than being tired and having problems finding a comfortable position to sleep things are going well. I am just resting up and taking it easy for now. I had a good long visit with a few friends yesterday and that always leaves me feeling good. Thank you Mike and Laura.

More later....

# Falling apart

July 21, 2014

Okay, this journaling is supposed to be about laying it all out there. I guess I knew the day would come when I would fall apart. The thing is I have always been independent and strong. I hate to be taken for a weakling, especially when my reputation is that of being a strong woman.

But sometimes the circumstances are not in your control and you have to trust and depend on others to help you. Even more so, you have to ask for help - not knowing exactly what it is that anyone can do for you. Maybe just listen, maybe just give you a hug and tell you that this too shall pass.

At the risk of making myself very vulnerable and feeling a bit like a weakling, if I am to be totally honest with my journaling, I need to include the days that aren't going so well just as much as those where I feel strong.

Chemo was easy compared to what I am going through right now. I don't know how it is that one little pill can make me feel worse than 16 rounds of chemo but if the past week or so is any indication then I'm in trouble.

This hormone/estrogen-blocking pill that I started taking on July 1 is called Letrozole. I was told that the most common side effects are hot flashes and joint aches. I wasn't too worried about this because I already have those symptoms. There are other side effects. My emotions are running crazy and I cry all the time for no reason. That is probably the most frustrating issue. My eyelashes and eyebrows have fallen out and the joint "aches" are actually pain, especially my right hip. I have a drain on the left side from surgery last week and can't sleep on my right side because of the hip pain, so that leaves me to my back which is not always comfortable.

So, I am not sleeping well which pretty much affects my whole day. I am also depressed - another lovely side effect of this pill. I have been trying to get a message to my doctor but haven't heard back yet for two days. I talked to my phone nurse and she told me to get in to see the doctor soon. She also said it may be recommended that I get on anti-depressants, NSAIDs and sleeping aids. I told her how I feel about taking pills and especially taking more pills to counteract the side effects of pills. She did get me in touch with a counselor though, so I am waiting for an appointment.

So, let me tell you how tired I am of all of this.

I'm tired of... crying for no reason, not having eyebrows or lashes, feeling ugly, feeling pain, feeling lonely and scared, feeling nothing at all.

This journey is supposed to be a life-changing event. So what is it I am supposed to change or do? I want to make a career change and I've been searching for answers but nothing is coming to me. People say to do what you are passionate about. The thing is I don't think I am passionate about anything. Lately I just don't care about much of anything. How can I not care about anything? What is wrong with me?

I am scared to make decisions in this state of mind.

I am not certain about the reconstructive surgery thus far. I was convinced after surgery last week that the port catheter was left in my neck. It still feels weird and it hurts. The nurse I talked to assured me that it was removed but that it didn't leave me feeling great.

I keep telling my doctor that I want smaller breasts. He says we need to fill the left up to match the right one. That doesn't make sense to me if I want a smaller end result. I know I need to trust him because this is what he does. I am almost to the point that I don't want any reconstruction at all but again, making that decision in my current state of mind wouldn't be wise.

I don't like being weak
I don't like complaining
I don't like who I am right now
I want to be normal again
I want to stop crying
I want to figure out what my purpose is in life.

I miss Jim. Some days I am just so mad at him for leaving me. I just want one more chance to talk to him. I don't know why I am having such a hard time processing his death. I am however very grateful to have Mike to talk to. Anytime I feel crappy, he listens and keeps me upbeat. I always walk away feeling like anything is possible in my life. I just don't want to wear him out with all my problems. He went through enough of that with Jim.

I honestly don't know what to do now. My supervisor at work is wonderful. She suggested more FMLA time if needed. It would be unpaid, so that's another worry for me but I am really struggling with work. I worked two hours this morning then took the rest of the day off sick. I went back to sleep for two hours and now I am trying to get some answers. When I first started treatment I felt like the doctors and nurses really cared. I got prompt attention and felt that they were going to take good care of me. I guess I just feel neglected. Is it because I've been doing so well for the past 7 months that they don't think I'm capable of having problems?

Well, there you have it... my down day. Hopefully there won't be too many of these types of journal entries because I really hate it. I hesitated to even include it but as I said, if I am to be honest in my journaling, it must include the good, the bad and the ugly.

On the up side... they say when things are falling apart in your life they may actually be falling in to place. I'd like to think that's what is happening to me now.

Drained again

July 24, 2014

The past few days have been better since my "Meltdown Monday."

I have to thank Connie for coming over and cheering me up... oh, and for the "sister pickles." I cracked them open today and they are yummy! It's been awhile since I've eaten pickles right out of the jar!

I've been busy with phone calls and follow ups, so here's the scoop... I have an appointment with a counselor on Monday. As much as it helps to talk to friends, I think it's time to add a professional to my list of supporters. It's a perk of the job anyway, so why not?

I have another appointment with the Nurse Practitioner next week on Survivorship. I also need to address issues regarding the dislocation of the right SC joint and that thing that runs up my neck since it still hurts.

I saw the plastic surgeon yesterday and we removed the dressings from surgery. The left breast is "unfurling" nicely per the doc. The drain remains since it's still putting out more than 30cc's per day. It will come out next week or sooner... I just need to get to that magic number!

When I asked about the line running up my neck on the right side, he said he didn't know what it was. He said he removed the port and catheter from the jugular but it was just below this area. I'm not sure what to think since this "thing" is still very prominent and hurts... more so now since surgery too, so I'm not convinced that it's not connected somehow. This whole "triangle" from the SC Joint to my shoulder to the neck has been a problem since the port surgery in January so I am just going to continue to ask until someone gives me a satisfactory answer!

I am also looking into taking some intermittent leave from work to accommodate more appointments and also allow me time to rest since I am not sleeping well at night. It's hard to believe how I breezed through chemo but now this one little pill is kicking my butt, if that's what this is. Hopefully we can get it under control or it will settle down over time. I have accepted the fact that I may need to take sleep aids or anti-depressants temporarily until I am "Laura" again instead of this hormonal maniac that seems to appear at any given moment.

For any guys reading this... you should count your lucky stars that you don't have hormonal issues like this!

That's about it. Feeling better for now... hope it lasts. Need to get outside and walk it off I think!

The drain remains mainly on the rainy plains

July 31, 2014

I realized that I am overdue for an update so here goes....

I saw the Counselor on Monday. I like her and she seems very competent. She says I am depressed but I am not sure I quite agree. I think I have bouts of depression but overall I feel I am doing well. I just need to know it's okay for me to have my little pity-parties now and then. I will continue to see her for a while just the same. We did discuss anti-depressants however; she said it's up to me and if I want to try to manage it with diet and exercise that's great.

I think part of the issue with my feeling down was that for about a week to 10 days post surgery I really didn't do much. I didn't go for my walks or hike, thinking I was doing the right thing so the drainage would slow down. Since I still have the drain in and it doesn't seem to matter how active I am I decided to get out and walk & hike again. Of course, that's when it decided to rain in Colorado for days on end so it's been a challenge to get out there! I did a 4 mile hike with a friend on Sunday and felt great. I also took a 3.5 mile walk on Monday. Believe me... as soon as this drain is out I am headin' for the hills!

I did start the "fill-er-up" process and got 50 cc's added to the expander. This helped to slow down the drain last time so hopefully it will work again this time. Two more fills and I'll be even up on both sides. Then I let things settle for a month or more. Probably more - I need a wee break!

So, on to yesterday and my Survivorship visit with the Nurse Practitioner. After discussing some of my little issues she spent time discussing how to get back to my life... either as I knew it or as I want it to be now. A reminder that every patient is different but she did assure me that this IS a life-changing event. My life will never be the same but that I will be okay. I guess I knew this but it helps to have someone tell you. The printout she gave me was from Live Strong - the organization that Lance Armstrong started when he was diagnosed with cancer. She made us all laugh when she said "Even though he was a cheater, he did start a good organization." So this visit was my official release more or less. I will still have follow up visits every three months for at least two years.

As for that stupid little pill... the symptoms seems to be settling down a bit so I am hopeful that I will tolerate it okay from now on. After researching the other options this one seems to have the fewest side effects. I can also say now that I've talked to the NP we cannot blame the meltdown on the pill alone. It was a cumulative effect and chemo can and does continue to cause side effects months afterwards. This makes sense but it's hard not to think that since I am no longer "in treatment" that my body will return to normal and I can pretend nothing ever happened! Again, the focus needs to continue to be on HEALING! I ask my friends to continue to help me remember this since I sometimes have delusions of grandeur!

The "thing" in my neck is believed to be a hemostasis or scar tissue. It doesn't seem to be of much concern and hopefully will heal with time. I also have an appointment to see an Ortho-Doc about the shoulder, elbow, and hand issues. Clearly I am NOT done with Doctors just yet!

I still feel big changes are coming my way and I am looking into my options. I don't plan to make any big decisions just yet. At least not until I've talked to my friends, family, counselor and anyone else who will listen to get some feedback. I want to jump into a RV and run away...

really I do! Please rest assured that I will not do this anytime soon and again, not without proper research and feedback.

I think my Counselor may have her work cut out for her trying to decide if I am crazy, depressed, or just plain weird!

Thank you all for caring so much. I guess that's appropriate since this is the "Caring" bridge! I feel very blessed to have the support and love from you all.

# The New Normal

August 4, 2014

It's unusual to think that after all I've been through this past 9-10 months that I find myself in a position to say that I want for nothing. That is to say there is nothing that I want or need in life right now. My life is full and complete and I have all that I need. That being said, I feel that I am in a place where I can make some changes. I've been wondering and contemplating what my next move would be.

So I have put in for more FMLA from work or a Leave of Absence. The FMLA actually isn't possible but I think I will still qualify for salary continuation. LOA might work better if it guarantees my job will still be here. My supervisor is so wonderful. She is helping me look into each option.

I have been feeling better and physically I am healing. It's the emotional and mental healing that is taking longer and seems to be the most frustrating to me. When I am out on walks or hikes I feel good and spending time with friends is great. Then I come back to work and sit at this computer and feel like I am chained to it and on a very strict schedule and all that weekend goodness unravels. The NP says my life is all about the "new normal" but I'm not sure what that is. I guess that in of itself is normal... NOT to know. It takes time to figure it all out. I never really thought of all of this as something that threatened my life but now that I've been told this and how all these feelings I am having are normal, it's taken on a bit of a new perspective. I can look normal and act normal on the outside but on the inside I am struggling.

I think the hardest part is to sit here and try to do a "normal" job when my mind is just not there. I don't even know what I want yet so how am I supposed to go on as normal in my work life? I write everything down because I know I won't remember! It's frustrating for me to say the least.

My counselor says I have a new view on what's important in life, which is very true. I am very grateful to have had this job and such a wonderful supervisor who has been a great advocate and friend. My heart is just not in this Monday-Friday/8-5 world anymore. I feel guilty for wanting to walk away from it all because if it hadn't been for this job and the benefits and my wonderful supervisor I wouldn't have been able to survive this. I feel like I owe it to the company to at least try to be a good employee again. Then again, I have given them 14 years of my best and maybe now it's okay to just take care of me?

Again, I have some big decisions ahead of me. I am hopeful that taking a bit more time off work will help me figure things out and get my head straight. The time I had off work before was spent mostly with doctor appointments, chemo and dealing with Jim's illness and passing. This is time that I need for healing myself. I understand that now and hope to gain some insight or at least just let my mind relax and live in the moment.

And so on with the "new normal"... whatever that may be for me. I think just being considered "normal" will be new for me!

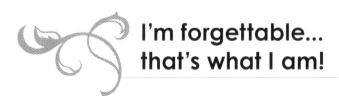

I'm forgettable... that's what I am!

August 11, 2014

Yes, the most frustrating thing I am experiencing lately is forgetfulness. I was already starting to get a little forgetful thanks to the aging process, but the chemo brain has made it even worse. I find myself writing down a LOT of things lately. Now if I can just remember where I put the paper that I wrote it on!

I have this week off work and have put in for additional leave. I don't know if it will be approved but it's increasingly difficult to focus and concentrate. Also very frustrating that it takes me 2-3 times longer and much more effort to do tasks that used to come so easily. I am told that all of this is normal though. Still frustrates me but nice to know that the medical professionals think I am normal. Okay that's not exactly what they said but that's what I heard!

I saw the Orthopedic Doctor today. He is not sure that my SC Joint is actually dislocated. He thinks it could be inflammation. Seven months after the port surgery it is still inflamed? He is going to look at my X-rays again and the CT Scan that I had, then talk to the previous doc I saw who said it was dislocated as well as the Radiologist. Then he will let me know what he decides is wrong with me. The shoulder he believes is bursitis and my hand & elbow pain he thinks is a pinched nerve. Yes, I've had a lot of trauma to my upper body over the past 7-8 months and the chemo could be to blame as well. Not sure if that holds true for the hand pain since it's gotten progressively worse for years now. I just hope to get some answers soon!

My legs however work just fine! I've been enjoying some great hikes over the past few days with friends. This year I've seen more wildflowers than I have since I moved here. It's so green and lush and gorgeous lately and I am so blessed to live here. I would probably be curled up in bed whining if I lived elsewhere!

So, the rest of my "week off" includes another visit with the plastic surgeon, my counselor, a nutritionist and the Nurse Practitioner. Throw in a few errands that need to be done and that about takes care of the week. I will update more, as I know it. For the time being it's still a roller coaster ride... but without the thrills of throwing my hands up in the air and screaming.

Thank you all for your support... I'm not sure which is worse, the physical healing or emotional and mental healing but I haven't heard the fat lady sing yet so I know it's not over!

And so on and so on....

August 15, 2014

It's been a busy week. I am on leave from the job again for about 8 weeks and it seems I am busier during my time off than I ever am when I am working!

I had several appointments this week. The Orthopedic Doctor was on Monday. The good news is that he doesn't seem to think the SC Joint is dislocated. He thinks my "bump" is inflammation, even 7-8 months after surgery! The shoulder is thought to be bursitis and the pain in my hand is thought to be due to a pinched nerve in my elbow. He is going to speak with the first doctor I saw (who told me the SCJ was dislocated) and also the radiologist then look at the X-ray and CT Scan again and get back to me. As he said, nothing is straight-forward with me after all I've had done to my body so he wants to be thorough!

I saw the plastic surgeon on Wednesday and got the last (hopefully) fill for now. He wants to see me again next week anyway just to make sure things are "unfurling" as well as he likes. He mentioned filling a bit more, to which I cringed! I already feel like I have these huge water balloons bouncing around on my chest so I will put up a bit of a fight if he wants to add more. We have to wait 6 weeks, take measurements and then wait another 6 weeks for the final surgery. That will put this into November and coincidentally almost one year from the date of my initial diagnosis.

Hard to believe these things go on as long as they do, but then again I will hopefully have many, many more years to enjoy life!

I also saw my Counselor on Wednesday. I really like her and even though I feel like I am making progress, I do want to keep seeing her. She has a great perspective on life and has been so helpful in suggesting ways for me to move on with my life and continue the healing process.

Thursday I saw the Nurse Practitioner for a follow up. I have to say I just really, really like her. She is so compassionate and caring. She is very interested in following how women cope with Calypso during and after treatment. She gave me a prescription sleep aid to try. I am still not sleeping all that well so she thinks this will help temporarily. We discussed the anti-depressants a bit more but for now I don't think I need them.

I also met with a nutritionist on Thursday and I really like her a lot too. I am so blessed to have such amazing support from so many different avenues during all of this. She is a natural foods chef already and going to school to be a nutritionist so I am her first Calypso patient. I am very hopeful to make changes in my diet and enjoy good, whole foods... you know, the kind that really pisses off that Calypso guy? I came home after visiting with her and threw out a lot of junk in my pantry! I'm ready for a change!

Friday, after a 6 mile bike ride, I went to visit a hospice patient. She is doing pretty good but didn't remember me from my first visit two weeks ago. That's not unusual though. She is an artist/painter and has her work displayed around the care center. She's a very sweet woman. The staff there are so good to the patients but it kinda breaks my heart a little too, seeing how these folks live out their remaining time.

So, that was my busy week. My weekend plans include a hike up the back side of Pikes Peak tomorrow and tubing down the river on Sunday. My counselor and NP both said to make sure I am enjoying time with friends and laughing a lot. Now that's a prescription I can totally get on board with!

I didn't realize how much I needed this time for myself. The leave that I had before was spent at appointments and chemo and dealing with Jim's passing. I didn't realize how exhausted I was after staying so strong and positive for so long. It was almost like I had to have someone tell me that it's okay to crash now and let the feelings come pouring out so I can start to rebuild again. So that's what I am doing. I am feeling better physically every day and gaining my strength back. The mental and emotional part is starting to get easier. I still am uncertain what the future holds but I am okay with that too. I don't need to have a plan right now. I just need to take care of me. Fortunately I have many friends who care and will help me along the way and all I have to do is ask!

Better days are ahead... fall is almost here, which is my favorite time of year. Time to go and marvel at the gorgeous colors of the aspens. It's very rejuvenating! If that doesn't lighten my heart, nothing will!

Bless you all for sharing and caring!

Remarkable!

August 20, 2014

My plastic surgeon says my left breast is unfurling "remarkably" well so I won't need any more filling. We just need to let it settle and do it's job, which is to relax the muscle around it and prepare it for the permanent implant. I must say I am happy with this news that my breast is cooperating. Nothing worse than boobs behaving badly!

I am also happy that I didn't have to fill more because I am going camping this weekend and that would have made sleeping even more uncomfortable. I did start taking the sleep aid and the first two nights I did sleep at least 6 hours before waking. The third night I only got about 4-5 before I woke and started tossing and turning. Not sure what's up with this sleep situation but I'm going to give it more time. Just like everything else I've been through it seems that time is what works. That would be ideal if I were a patient person. Maybe that's the lesson I am supposed to be learning... patience!

I haven't heard back from the Ortho-doc but I left a message. My right hand isn't hurting as much as it did for the past two weeks but it's still achy so I'd like to know what is going on there too. Same with the SC Joint and shoulder. I know he said nothing is straight forward with me but I've never considered myself a "woman of mystery" really!

So, I am trying to keep myself occupied in the meantime. I am walking or hiking every day and that helps a lot with my emotions & moods, not to mention gaining my strength and stamina back! Just being in nature is so healing. The camp out this weekend should be fun. We have a group of about 26 people going to Turquoise Lake near Leadville and that should be beautiful. Just what the doctor ordered!

Until next time....

 # Better than therapy!

August 25, 2014

I just spent the weekend camping and hiking at Turquoise Lake over near Leadville, CO. I swear it's better than therapy!

The Outdoor/Hiking group that I organize got about 27 people signed up and we all headed over for a camping weekend. Sitting around the campfire at night, listening to a couple guys strumming on the guitars and sipping on some wine. Life is good!

We hiked to Timberline Lake on Saturday and even though it rained a bit on us, we thoroughly enjoyed it. Of course once we got back to camp the sun came out! I rode the bike a little, hung out at camp and just socialized.

On Sunday, Mary and I went over to look for a hike called Hagerman Tunnel. We didn't see anything labeled but found a trailhead nearby so decided just to get out and stretch the legs before heading home. We walked along this very straight, long (old railroad) trail and just as we were wondering to continue or turn back a couple came up a hill and told us which way to go to the tunnel and lake!

We followed them for a short climb then they told us about the loop and they headed one way and we headed the other way. It was one of the best hikes I've done this year... maybe even to date. It was just gorgeous and hiking with someone who appreciates the simple beauty of Gods country made it even better. Thank you so much Mary - your company was delightful! We did run into the couple again on the other side of the loop and thanked them for the "tip."

I posted a new photo of me at Hagerman Lake. I'm rather pleased with it since many people have told me lately how good I look (and it isn't just the hair)! I didn't realize how much I needed this time off just for me!

So, we ended up leaving the area around 3:00pm and got back to the Springs around 6:00pm. I made a short stop at home to unload some things and went to pick up the bunnies. My house just isn't the same without those little furballs here. I slept very well Sunday night. After sleeping in a tent and in the car, it was nice to shower and sleep in my own bed! I plan to head west again in a week or so and just take a little solo time to see more of this amazing state I live in.

I realized a few things today...

- How many good, kind, generous and caring people I have in my life.
- How precious and fleeting a moment can be.
- How to let go (I am still a "work in progress" on this one but I'm getting better)!
- How blessed I am to live in such a gorgeous place.
- How much I enjoy living a simple life.

I had no problem at all "unplugging" for the weekend and just enjoying living in the moment and enjoying time with friends out in nature. I think the world would have so few problems if everyone would just "take a hike!"

The famous saying in Colorado is "Life is Good." That pretty much sums up how I feel right now in this moment. I am very grateful, very blessed and very content. Thank you Lord for this wonderful life!

Here I am at Haggerman Lake, enjoying the day.

Grateful is an understatement

August 31, 2014

I feel so grateful and so blessed today. I did a hike yesterday that was double any hiking I've done since last October. I knew going in that it was going to be tough and test my limits and it certainly was and it certainly did! The grand total was twelve miles and 1500 feet elevation gain, which was mostly on the way back. And that was between 10,300-11,800 feet! I am so grateful to those who went with me and helped to (literally) push me along and encourage me. I am also grateful that I was able to get out of bed this morning!

I went to a support group meeting on Thursday evening and heard stories from a few other survivors who are really struggling. Their problems extended beyond just the treatment or the disease. Made me feel really strange, like I shouldn't be there since I am doing so well. But as one of them told me "Maybe they need your support." Well that's an interesting viewpoint now isn't it? But I had to ask myself… am I in a position to support someone else?

I also made a visit to a hospice patient along with another volunteer. She was so happy to have visitors and the other volunteer was really good with her. I found it very helpful to watch their interaction and hope that I can be that good one day. I guess it just takes time to really get comfortable with it. The other volunteer said most people in nursing homes rarely get visitors so I'm glad to take a little time to visit.

So to say I am grateful seems like an understatement. I feel like I have been given a gift. The past few months and especially the past few weeks have been very enlightening for me. I feel like a whole new world has been opened up to me. It's like I've earned a degree in "life" during this journey. Maybe I had become too complacent in my day-to-day life or I wasn't fulfilling my destiny. I'm still uncertain of what's in store for me but my eyes are certainly wide open now and there is a heightened awareness. My journey is far from being over... maybe it's just the beginning.

Remembering Jim

September 3, 2014

Just a short note about my day today. Mike and I decided rather spontaneously to take time today to spread some of Jim's ashes around the local places that he designated in the Springs. I was honored to help Mike do this though I thought it would be difficult for me emotionally. It was anything but that.

We started out with a spot on a trail behind Walmart on 8th Street where he found Tasha, his beloved cat of 16 years. We had mixed Tasha's ashes with Jim's for this occasion. Next we went to one of the houses that he lived in when he first had Tasha and spent lots of time with her on the back deck. As we pondered how to proceed, we noticed a cat sitting on the ledge of the house. We took this as a good sign! So we knocked on the door and the woman that answered was very kind. When we told her our mission and that the previous owner had passed, she said "Jim?" She wasn't even the one who bought the house from Jim. It was the owner before her! I am not sure how she knew him but we were not surprised. He left an impression on so many people.

Next we stopped at his most recent house and left some ashes there in the yard. Again, there was a cat in the yard! This was getting kinda spooky! Finally we drove up Gold Camp Road to High Drive. Jim rode this daily as his "workout" routine. It was gorgeous and, as Mike and I concluded would be unbelievably challenging on a bike! Exactly what made Jim tick... a physical challenge! We met a few cyclists on their way up or down and we both could just picture any of them as Jim.

We spread his ashes on small bluff that overlooks the Broadmoore hotel through the valley. Looking the other way were the rocks above Helen Hunt falls, so there was beauty all around!

We stopped at Helen Hunt falls and did a quick "selfie" which I have included here. It was an amazing day spent with a good friend to honor the wishes of our dear Jim. Mike and I both felt so honored to be able to do this and finally get Jim out where he would want to be... among the rocks and trees and hillsides.

We laughed a lot about many of Jim's quirks and memories and what we loved about him. Though he no longer walks among us, he is now everywhere around us. It was such a wonderful day so I wanted to share it here with you all.

With Mike at Helen Hunt Falls

Going "Somewhere"

September 12, 2014

You may want to get out a Colorado map to follow along on this story!

September 9 at 7:30am
My car is packed up and ready to head west. Destination.... TBD.

I arrived at Buena Vista around 10:00am. The weather was gorgeous going over but clouds were surrounding the pass. The forecast in Crested Butte was heavy rain for the night, so I decided to pass on Cottonwood pass! After consulting the map the car headed south. I'll just get Crested Butte on the return.

It rained and/or misted most of the day as I headed over Monarch Pass and into Gunnison. I was still enjoying it and found myself smiling a lot that day. When I got to Gunnison I consulted the map again and found Black Canyon nearby. That sounded good to me, so I continued heading west and the drive was gorgeous. On my right were rock cliffs and on the left was Blue Mesa reservoir. I got to Black Canyon and was absolutely amazed at its beauty. The canyon is narrow and deep - around 2700 feet at the highest point. Running through the bottom was the Gunnison River. I could actually hear it at the top at some points too!

I spent a few hours there hiking and taking LOTS of photos. I thought about camping there but when I looked at the map again Ouray popped out at me and it wasn't far. It was only around 4:30pm so why not? I stopped in Montrose for a fill up the tank and headed south. The drive was very pretty with several 14ers coming into view... Mt. Sneffles, Uncompahgre and Wetterhorn. I passed through Ridgeway and onto Ouray. This town is nestled in a small valley surround by mountains. It's a very quaint mountain town.

I wasn't sure about staying the night so I started up Million Dollar Highway towards Silverton. It only took a few miles for me to decide I did not want to navigate that drive. It's a winding highway along a canyon wall and the sun would be setting within the hour. So back to Ouray, I passed Yankee Boy Basin. If the 14ers didn't make me think of Jim, this certainly did. I read about it in his trip reports. This was his playground and the thought of him made me smile.

I drove through Ampitheatre Campground, which was on switchback road high above Ouray. It was pretty but very secluded and just didn't feel right. I passed some cabins on the way in so I stopped but the office was closed. That left one more option before heading back to the State Park in Ridgeway. There was a KOA campground just outside Ouray and they had a cabin available. Perfect! I was settled in by 7:30pm and in bed asleep by 9:30pm. What a day!

September 10
I woke at 7:00am and left the campground by 8:00am. As I drove away from Ouray the rear view mirror showed low clouds sitting in the valley. It was very pretty.

I stopped at Ridgeway State Park and walked around and took some photos. On to Montrose and a stop to look at my options. I had written a few ideas down for today which included going up to Delta and perhaps a stop at Sweitzer State Park. After looking again, I decided to head back east a bit to continue the loop on Hwy 92, which would take me to the north rim of Black Canyon. It was a beautiful drive and another winding road along the canyon wall. I stopped at the north rim and hiked a short while, took photos then moved on.

Hwy 133 took me up to Paonia State Park but it didn't look all that interesting so I came back the few miles and headed over Kebler Pass. It didn't say how far to Crested Butte but no matter, I drove on. It was mostly dirt road but a good road. The aspens were just starting to turn which made it a very pretty drive. The CD I had playing was by Enya "Who can say where the road goes? Where the day flows? Only time." My feelings exactly!

I pulled in to Crested Butte around 4pm. I walked around the town and it was another very quaint mountain town but I just wasn't feeling that's where I wanted to stay the night.

I topped off the tank and headed over Cottonwood pass towards Buena Vista. Another beautiful pass and the views from the top of the pass were stunning. I walked around the top and hiked up to a better vantage point for photos then on to Buena Vista.

So, now I arrive in Buena Vista about 6:30-6:45pm. I stopped and had an ice cream cone and consulted the map again. I had already been south and just came from the west. I could go north to Leadville and stay the night. That would be really cold camping at over 10,000 feet and the weenie in me said "nah." My other option was to drive home and shower and sleep in my own bed. By the time I finished eating my ice cream cone I had decided to be homeward bound. I felt that I had done quite a bit in those two days and the mountains aren't going anywhere. I'll be back.

I do enjoy hiking and traveling with friends. Traveling alone is a bit of a challenge. Traveling alone with no plan is a fine line between adventuresome and crazy. The thing is that I didn't have to plan anything... it all just unfolded there in front of me and I was happy with every turn I made. I thought to myself "This is how I want to live my life... just let it unfold."

I put over 700 miles on the car and saw some amazingly gorgeous places and collected a lot of information. I smiled a lot, talked to folks along the way and found myself giving thanks to God for allowing me to live is such a scenic place. More than once my eyes teared up, filled with gratitude. I may have cut my trip short just a bit but I had seen plenty and dare I say I might have had "mountain overload?"

During the trip I finished a book called "The Untethered Soul" by Michael A. Singer. The last part talks about the decision to be happy. In life we can *decide* to be happy or not happy. It really is just that simple. No matter what life hands you, it's still your decision on how you react and whether or not you're going to let it make you unhappy.

I've had my ups and downs with Calypso but in the end I find that I am happy. I don't know if I would be in this blissful state if I had not taken that journey this past year. I highly recommend the book. I highly recommend taking a trip alone and I very highly recommend being happy!

This photo is at Black Forest of the Gunnison National Park.

Falling behind

September 22, 2014

Looks like I've fallen a little behind in my journaling so it's time for an update.

When we last heard from Laura, she had just finished a solo sight seeing journey around south-central Colorado. The week following my trip was rather uneventful. I did get to hike with my friend Audrey up to Raspberry Mountain. That is a fairly tough hike with a lot of climbing but we took our time and enjoyed the perfect weather day. We talked and laughed a lot and she taught me all about different types of pine trees. Not that I will remember any of it, but that woman really knows her pine trees!

The aspen colors weren't at peak yet that day but this past weekend made up for it. I went with a group of twelve over to the Aspen/Snowmass area. We had two condos reserved for two nights. The drive over Independence pass was just gorgeous. It was hard to be the driver when I really wanted to be the gawker! Still, when there is that much color you see it all around. The drive over was especially entertaining with Amy hanging out the front window taking pictures and Tara rolling around from side to side in the back and out the sun roof snapping away!

Other than calling it "Aspen gold" I cannot think of a word that describes it and the camera shows the beauty but really doesn't do it justice. I am so grateful to have been able to witness the colors in their prime and in an area where it is so abundant.

We did a short hike on Friday near Snowmass Village where we were staying. In winter, this is a popular ski area. Saturday was the main event as we took the bus up to hike to Crater Lake and see Maroon Bells. I included a photo of me here at Maroon Lake with the Bells in the background. These are two of the 54 Colorado 14er peaks. This area is the most photographed place in Colorado... and you can see why. I found myself smiling a lot on the trail and also tearing up just a bit, filled with gratitude to be fortunate enough to do this. I may still be "under construction" from the waist up, but thank God my legs are working well and I'm gaining my strength back!

On Sunday some of us took the gondola up to Aspen Mountain at 11,212 feet. It was a little drizzly but no complaints here. The views were still awesome and I didn't even break a sweat getting to the top! After doing some touristy stuff in town, we had lunch and headed back home.

It's hard to find words to describe the weekend... it was the most scenic trip I've done in ages, the people were so much fun to hang out with and I left feeling relaxed and content with myself and with life.

So, today I am back to reality. I saw an orthopedic doctor for the hand pain and numbness I've had. He is ordering a nerve test, thinking it's a nerve in either my hand or elbow or both. I asked him what a nerve test involves and he said "needles." I have to admit, that "unnerved" me a bit! I've had my share of needles this year for sure, but when you combine needles & nerves, I just don't think it's going to be pleasant. Still, if it gets results I guess it's worth it.

I see another Ortho-doc on Wednesday for the shoulder and SC joint issue that's been going on since January. That could possibly be a nerve issue too and maybe it's all connected or related so we can get it all resolved in one fell swoop! I know, I am such an optimist... but wouldn't that be really great?

I see my plastic surgeon this week too so hopefully we can order up my new boobs and get the final surgery scheduled. Time to see what the booby prize is for all of this.

I think I am starting to see the beginning of the end. It's hard to believe sometimes that this has taken up a year of my life. I charged right through the physical part and chemotherapy. The mental and emotional healing is much harder to deal with but I think I am making progress. I've always had a positive attitude and feel that I am a strong and independent woman so working on the mind and emotions is perplexing and frustrating at times. It's also hard to put myself first and tell people no if I just don't feel like doing something but my counselor told me it's okay to have boundaries. I've put it to practice a few times already and the result has been a lighter and happier feeling so I guess it's an important part of my emotional healing.

I hope to see more fall colors in the next week or two before the leaves fall... but even after they fall, I will be *walking on gold* so it's all good. There just isn't a bad season here in Colorado. They all have something wonderful to offer. Winter sends folks to the slopes for skiing (or tubing in my case). Spring's thaw fills the streams that we hike along so we can enjoy the babbling brooks. Summer flowers send me frolicking like a fool and the fall colors just prove what an amazing artist God is!

Thanks for reading all... the journey may be coming to an end soon but I still have a lot to say so stay tuned!

At Maroon Lake with Maroon Bells in the distance. Life just doesn't get any better than this!

Fall Color Fever

September 27, 2014

This past week has been absolutely amazing. I have been able to get out almost every day and see the fall colors. I believe I have a severe case of Fall-Color-Fever. From my list of doctors, I'm not sure which I would need to see for this condition but I don't believe I really want a cure! It's been absolutely crucial to my well-being and I am again grateful that my legs are still in fine working order.

I drove a circle around Pikes Peak on Tuesday and stopped at Mueller State Park and hiked a few miles before heading home. This was another of those days that I grabbed a map, my hiking shoes and snacks and just headed out the door without a plan. These types of days have proven that life certainly is worth living in the moment!

On Thursday I went over to hike Pancake Rocks with my friend Laura. I called it a Laura-Laura day. This hike is one of the most popular on the Front Range during the aspen peak season. I'm just glad we were able to go on a weekday! It was a difficult hike but we just took our time and it was very much worth the effort!

Friday I went up to Woodland Park and spent the morning with another friend, Kathy. We went to the farmers market then hiked with a small group up near Divide. Afterwards we came back to her house and had lunch and I headed back to the Springs for physical therapy.

Saturday I went hiking through Emerald Valley and up to Duffields Meadow with some good friends. It was a perfect weather day and the aspens were still peaking. I feel so absolutely blessed to have good friends to spend time with right now. It feels good to relax and laugh and just enjoy great company. Dawn is hosting a get together this week for some of my gal pals, so more relaxing & enjoyment time to come. I feel lighter, healthier and happier now than I have in a very long time.

As far as the medical update... my SC joint is, in fact, dislocated. I may also have a nerve being pinched in my neck. The physical therapy should help with this but I will also be getting a MRI to make sure there is nothing else going on along the clavicle bone. A few more weeks and one more surgery and I can hopefully close out this tab and move on. Check please! On second thought, I probably don't even want to know the cost of all this. Thank God I have good insurance!

This week will be down to the business of making some appointments and getting scheduled for these procedures. Ah, yes... reality.

Pancake Rocks on the west side of Pikes Peak.

With Louise, Pam, Anne, Dawn and Deb.

Abundance

October 1, 2014

Me at Cascade Falls near St. Elmo, CO.

Abundance... it's been on my mind a lot over the past few months. I had a friend do numerology for me and she said the next year would be one of abundance. I think most people including myself (initially) think of this in a monetary sense but the more I think of it, I realize it is so much more.

I took a drive out west again yesterday to explore and hike. Though I didn't get to hike as much as I thought, the drive time was good thought processing time. There were still a lot of aspens to view and I realized something. Just as these leaves are changing, I too have been changing. Perhaps that is why I've been drawn to them.

I have a birthday coming up in a few weeks. Last year, it was 9 days after my birthday that I discovered the lump in my breast. At some point early in my diagnosis, I wrote a note to myself and sealed it up and put it away. On the envelope I wrote: "to be opened in October 2014." I have seen it now and then and it got me to thinking when exactly to open it. I think my birthday will be the perfect time to open it.

I was telling Mike about it and we discussed what a very cool thing this is to do. Instead of a new years resolution, maybe we should all write a note to ourselves and stuff it away and open it on New Years Eve. I don't remember exactly what I wrote but I believe it was something to do with where I would be at this point in my life. I will share it here after I have opened it.

So back to abundance. As I was driving yesterday I continue to just "live in the moment" and appreciate things as they come and not to worry too much about the future. When I tell friends I don't know if I want to go back to work and they ask me what I want to do, I reply: "I don't know." This is truly a leap of faith for me. The more I think about it, the more I know that it's just about having faith that God has a plan for me and it will be revealed to me as I am ready for it.

My friend Debi gave me a book of daily devotionals called "Jesus Calling." After spending the day driving, thinking, observing, appreciating and contemplating my life I opened up to the September 30 page and here is what I read...

"I am perpetually with you, taking care of you. That is the most important fact of your existence. I am not limited by time or space; My presence with you is a forever promise. You need not fear the future, for I am already there. When you make that quantum leap into eternity, you will find Me awaiting you in heaven. Your future is in my hands; I release it to you day by day, moment by moment. Therefore, do not worry about tomorrow."

"I want you to live this day *abundantly*, seeing all there is to see, doing all there is to do. Don't be distracted by future concerns. Leave them to Me! Each day of life is a glorious gift, but so few people know how to live within the confines of today. Much of their energy for abundant living spills over the timeline into tomorrow's worries or past regrets. Their remaining energy is sufficient only for limping through the day, not for living it to the full. I am training you to keep your focus on My presence in the present. This is how to receive abundant Life, which flows freely from My throne of grace."

This pretty much sums up how I am living my new life, my second life if you will. It's sometimes hard for friends to understand that I don't have a plan for what to do next... and I am perfectly okay with that! I have been letting life simply unfold before me and what I am finding is abundance. I have good friends, beautiful places to visit, peace in my life and faith & hope for the future. That is truly an abundant life.

Dances at Moonrise

October 3, 2014

I had a really amazing day yesterday so of course I have to share with ya'all!

My friend Mike and I finally coordinated our schedule with Audrey (a long time friend of Jim's) and did our trip to Glenwood Springs to spread some of his ashes at a house he owned about 15 years ago.

Audrey, Mike and I at Indy Pass.

I met Mike at his house at 8am and then we picked up Audrey at her house in Divide around 9am and headed west. It was a great drive as we shared memories and stories of Jim. I continue to learn more about him all the time. Audrey and her husband have known Jim for quite some time and he taught her how to fly fish, which is now a passion of hers. It's really great to hear her stories of Jim. One of the most recent stories is how she put a patio chair on her deck that was his and shortly after this, a deer and her two twin fawns have been hanging out at her house. She said in 23 years they have never had deer in the back yard!

So, we decided to take Independence pass over that way. There was quite a bit of snow but still a lot of fall color. The "up" side was snowier than the "down" side. I always love going over that pass. It's the highest paved pass in Colorado. It was pretty darn cold up top though! I've included a photo of us at the overlook.

We had an old address that I got from some photo envelopes along with pictures of the house. The only problem was, we weren't able to find it in advance on google maps or mapquest. We decided to just "wing it" and count on Jim to guide us. We drove through the subdivision, which was now a gated community but still not many houses in the area. After searching up and down two streets we saw a deer and her two fawns. We took this as a good sign! Just as we were about to drive out of the gated community, we spotted the house number on the slab of rock. It was the very first house as we came in to the gated community! How did we miss that?

We drove down the driveway and the house was exactly as shown in the photos. It was exhilarating and eerie at the same time. We rang the bell and nobody answered. There was a truck in the driveway with Minnesota plates. Audrey is originally from MN so we took this also as a good sign! We went around the back and were blown away by the views. The house overlooked Capital and Snowmass - two 14er peaks. Jim lived there long before he got the 14er-fever but still, it brought tears to my eyes. We spread some ashes out past the yard and Audrey found a wire stick-like-figure. We propped him up, called him Jim and left him to gaze at the mountains. We also left the photos along with a note on the door for the owners... just in case they knew Jim. You never know... he made quite an impression on people that he encountered! We also did a quick "selfie" at his house - photo included.

We continued on to Glenwood Springs and had lunch at the Denver hotel. I'd eaten there before and it was just as good as I remembered. As we were leaving Glenwood, we saw the signs for Hanging Lake. Neither Mike nor Audrey had ever been and it was a fairly short hike, so we made a detour and stretched our legs a bit. It was so exciting for me to show them this little gem tucked away in the canyon. During the summer it's usually packed with tourists but today at 4pm, there were very few cars. I think I may need to seriously think of this type of "work" for my future. I so enjoy showing people all the beautiful places to visit in Colorado! I've included a photo of us at hanging lake.

With Mike and Audrey at Hanging Lake.

As we were coming down from the top of the canyon, the moon was up already. I thought of Jim, since his alter ego was "dancesatmoonrise." What a perfect ending to a perfect day.

It was nearly 6pm when we left, so we knew it was going to be a "dark" drive home. We headed east on I-70 and then took the Tennessee pass over through Leadville. It was such a pretty drive and we saw a moose on the side of the road! He looked like he was going to cross but saw us and changed his mind. We stopped the car and looked back and he was back in the middle of the road. Quite a big boy too! It was a little too dark to take a photo, but that was my first sighting of REAL wildlife in Colorado!

It was a long day but such a wonderful feeling to honor Jim's requests and get him back out where he would want to be. I am also blessed with two new friends and I have Jim to thank for that. Mike has become such a trusted friend and the more I get to know Audrey, the more I like her.

I continue to live each day and just try to appreciate the moment and the people I am with. I worry less about tomorrow or the future. Days like this just make me believe all the more that I am on the right path and letting it all unfold before me is working out pretty darn good!

Selfie at Jim's old house

 # A Pinch of this and a pinch of that

October 10, 2014

I thought it was time for another medical update now that I've got a bit more information. I had such a lovely day on Monday (she says sarcastically). I had an appointment with my counselor in the morning (a teary-eyed session) and a nerve test after lunch (needles and nerves) and then a visit with a Psychiatrist in the afternoon (more tears). At least I got it all done in one day but man, was I exhausted!

The nerve test showed that I have pinched nerves in my wrist and elbow, so I've got Carpal Tunnel and Cubital Tunnel to thank for the pain and numbness in my right hand. She said the only thing that would correct it is surgery so now we just have to see if that will come before or after my final breast surgery on November 4th. I will be following up with the hand Doc next week I hope.

For the dislocated SC joint, I started physical therapy and it was okay at first but then everything started hurting and I have been hearing more "popping" noises along the clavicle bone, so my physical therapist said to stop for now and follow up with the doctor. I am getting a MRI on Tuesday so maybe that will reveal some answers to this mystery that has had everyone stumped since January!

I really need this issue resolved since it interferes with my ability to carry a backpack. Not that it has prevented me from hiking... I just use my waist pack. However, with winter coming up I will need to carry more stuff. I have continued to hike with friends and get out and enjoy the mountains and the colors and fresh air. I do believe that is where the famous Colorado saying came from... "Life is Good." It had to be someone out on a trail, in nature, looking at the trees and the mountains. Makes everything else just disappear and you realize how insignificant some things really are. Right there in that moment, you realize... Life is Good. And no matter what I have thrown at me, I will continue to believe that for the remainder of my own life... it's all good.

So, I was required to see a Psychiatrist in order to extend my leave from work for a few more weeks. I have never seen a Psychiatrist so I wasn't sure what to expect. He was very clinical, a bit peculiar and asked me a boatload of questions while taking lots of notes. If I hesitated on my answer, he turned and leaned in towards me as if I were about to give him the answers to the universe. It was a little weird. He believes that I am not sleeping well (duh) and the Restoril that I am currently taking to help me sleep can act as a depressant. He prescribed something else for sleep along with an anti-depressant. I am to follow up with him in a few weeks to see how it's going.

In the meantime, I spent a couple hours with my nutritionist and she mentioned that I might want to see if there is a way to check my melatonin levels. That certainly made a lot of sense to me. I have a follow up with my Oncologist soon so I will ask if we can do that. Wouldn't that be great if I could just take some organic melatonin and sleep well and not be a pill-popper? My nutritionist really knows her stuff. She has had health issues in the past, which is why she wanted to study nutrition. She researches the crap out of everything before proceeding, so I trust the information she provides. I am very fortunate to have her helping me.

So, I think that about wraps up my update. Quite enough excitement for now and it's time for me to get back on the trails anyway.

Until next time....

Now where was I?

October 19, 2014

I just realized it's been over a week and no updates. There really isn't a lot to tell except well, I am a year older than I was when I wrote the last entry. I had a fun birthday hike in the morning with Bobbie and Bella (the dog) and then celebrated with about 30 or so friends at Jose Muldoon's downtown in the evening. It was a lot of fun and I even drank a shot! The waiter kept asking if he could get me a birthday shot and after about an hour of him asking I finally succumbed. It was a Pineapple Upside down shot, which tasted like a pineapple smoothie with a kick! Not too bad really, and besides I earned this!

Last week I started a 4-week class called New Visions: Career Opportunities after retirement. Now, I know I am not retired but it seems to be geared towards what I am looking for... a new direction for my new life. I still don't know what I want to be when I grow up but hopefully this will help. The teacher has great credentials and I like her so we'll see what happens. And for plan B, as my sister Eva always reminds me... there's still Clown College! Ha!

I did have the MRI scheduled for last week but when I got there they said I couldn't get it because of the temporary implants (they have metal in them). I told the person who made the appointment but apparently that didn't compute! So, now I have to see what the doctor wants to do... we can do a CT Scan now or wait until after my surgery then do the MRI. Either way, I am in limbo again on the SC Joint thingy. UGH!

I have still been hiking a lot and went to see Chihuly at the Denver Botanic Gardens on Saturday with a few friends. Absolutely gorgeous work and the weather was perfect. I've included a photo... hard to pick just one from all I took! Between the gardens, flowers and his works I took about 200 photos that day!

More hiking this week and more appointments too, so until then....

Happy Trails!

One of many of the Chihuly Exhibits at the Denver Botanical Gardens.

The Letter

October 20, 2014

I actually forgot to open my letter on my birthday!

I wrote this note to myself on January 18, 2014. This would be just a few days after my first chemo treatment. I wrote on the envelope "To be opened October 2014" and stuck it away. I just read it today and wanted to share it here. You would have thought I wrote this today. Guess I believed this is how the year would go and it came to be! I think this is a good idea and maybe we should all do this on New Years Eve. Write a letter to yourself and tuck it away until the next NYE. See what happens!

October 2014

What a year it's been thus far. I survived chemo, radiation and the loss of a dear friend. I had no idea the strength it would take but with love, prayers and support from family and friends... I survived! These lessons in life that we learn... some are fairly easy, some are a struggle, but each one shapes us into who we are to become.

My Calypso was not something I ever imagined would happen to me. It was a process that opened my eyes to a new future. I tried to stay positive throughout the journey for I knew there was a reason.

My dear friend Jim was also diagnosed with cancer but the terminal kind. I loved him and I miss him every day. He was absolutely the most fascinating, extraordinary man I've ever known. And because of his generosity I am able to have a better life and pass on that generosity.

Yes, it's been quite a year... almost to the day when I first heard that word... cancer. I chose to call it Calypso... sounds much better. I have another birthday coming up and the holidays are right around the corner... my favorite time of year. I have much to be thankful for - my health, friends and family who care, a new life and memories of my loved one Jim.

"It's a wonderful life"

A tale of two surgeries

October 25, 2014

October is almost over and the holidays will be here before we know it. I am very much looking forward to Thanksgiving this year. I have much to be thankful for, including some pretty amazing people in my life and my health. Yes, my health is returning to almost normal and by the time Thanksgiving arrives I will hopefully have the last of my surgeries behind me.

I have my final breast reconstruction scheduled for November 4th. According to my plastic surgeon, this one is "easy peasy lemon squeezy." Okay, not his words exactly but that's how I understood it. No drains this time and much easier recovery. We'll just take out these water balloons that I've been carrying on my chest for nearly a year and put in the FM500's! That is actually what they are called. I'm told patients hate the temporary ones but the permanent ones more closely resemble breast tissue. I'll reserved judgement until they are in place.

I have another surgery two weeks after this one. November 18th I will have surgery to fix the carpal tunnel and cubital tunnel in my right hand/ elbow. I have mild carpal tunnel in my left hand but the right is moderate and both wake me up during the night with numbness and some pain so hopefully this will help me sleep better once it's done.

As far as the sleep goes, I have decided to give the Melatonin a try rather than keep taking more sleep aids. I really hate taking drugs and the original prescription the Psychiatrist gave me made me groggy... so he gave me another one - Lunesta. I don't know if this one has the same issues as Ambien. I think Ambien is the one that has people "sleep driving." If the Melatonin doesn't work then I might give it a try. I wonder if I hide my car keys from myself before I go to bed... will my sleep self remember where I hid them should I try to sleep drive?

So, that's the latest and greatest for now. I'll be glad to get this year over with. I'm sure I've stated that before but it bears repeating, right?

Off now for more hiking.... grateful to have two good, working legs!

Going out on a HIGH note!

Nov 2, 2014

The end is coming! The end is coming!

No, not the worlds end... just the journey that I've been on this year. I've got a few milestones coming up... my final breast surgery is Tuesday. Bring on the FM500's! Then December 3rd will mark my first anniversary of being Calypso free.

To celebrate I climbed my first and only 14er of the year. I wasn't even sure I could do this and up until a few days before I wasn't sure I even wanted to try! See, Jim and Steve (a fellow mountaineer who passed away the year before Jim) started this "Winter Welcomer" tradition. Last year I wasn't able to go and it was Jim's last 14er. That in of itself made me want to go this year. I also needed to do it for myself... to prove that I have my strength back and that I am indeed an "overcomer." Plus it seemed to be a nice "finisher" for me... going out on a VERY high note!

With Britt and Mike on top of Quandary Peak – 14, 265 feet.

So, I was up at 5:00am on Saturday morning and over to get Mike and Fred and head west. Thankfully Mike drove so I was able to relax on the way over. We arrived at the trailhead around 7:35am and got geared up to go. Hit the trail just after 8:00am. I admit more than once, I asked myself "What the hell are you doing?" I tried not to focus on the summit. Instead I made small goals all the way… first just get out of tree line (12,000 feet) then get to that ridge (12,500) and the next ridge (13,000). Next just get across the ridge to the start of that last steep "up." That last steep section is about 1200 feet elevation gain in under a mile. I stopped a lot and Mike did a little pulling and pushing along the way. We summited right before noon which was my goal. Total elevation gain was 3325 feet. It was quite the accomplishment and I just cried when I got to the top. We saw our friend Britt and there were hugs all around. It was a very emotional and successful climb.

What most people don't think about on these types of climbs is that gaining the summit is only half the battle. Getting down can be about as difficult as getting up. It's just easier on the lungs going down. It took me almost 4 hours to climb and over 2 to get down. A long, tiring day but I had a silly smile on my face all the way down!

My knees were reminding me this morning that I am 56 years old and shouldn't be doing things like that. I just smiled and said "Get used to it knees... I've only just begun my comeback!"

I am so very grateful. This year has been unlike any other in my life. I struggled a little, learned a lot and shared the journey with some very good friends. I think when you experience a major, life changing event you find out real quick who your true friends really are. I've been blessed with many - old and new. Words cannot express my thanks for those who were there for me. I know you couldn't all be here to hold my hand but I know you were there in spirit and prayers. Thank you from the bottom of my heart. I don't think I would have been able to stand on a mountain top without your support!

Standing atop Quandary... as far as I am concerned I am on top of the world! Appreciating Gods masterpiece and feeling grateful to be alive!

Ending on a high note would be the obvious place to end this book. However, I still have a bit more to say. There's a shocker, right?

Climbing a 14er certainly was the high point of this year for me. It was a perfect ending to a less-than-perfect year.

The remainder of the year was much less eventful. However, I did include a few more stories before wrapping it all up and sticking it under the tree!

Brand new knockers

Nov 5, 2014

Well, I had my final breast reconstruction yesterday and everything went about as well as it could have. My FM500's are looking pretty good, if I do say so myself. It's nice not to have those water balloons on my chest any longer. These permanent implants are made of a solid material so no more sloshing around!

The Doc was a little late yesterday but other than that, everything went very well. The only thing was surgery was supposed to be at 1:00pm and I was really hungry and the tummy was grumbling all the while checking in and prepping. I think we were only about 1/2 hour late... so a bit more grumbling and then it was show time. I got some good drugs before we left around 4-4:30pm and had a nice rest both there and when I got home.

This morning I got up and went for a short walk. I feel pretty darn good too! There is just a little tightness in the chest area but no pain, so that's good. I have no restrictions really other than not lifting more than 10 pounds for a while. The incisions look pretty small too. As Dawn said "cut-cut, pull-pull, stuff-stuff, sew-sew." That pretty much sums it up!

Thank you all for the thoughts and prayers. I'll be taking it easy for a few days with just some easy walks and short outings. Next milestone is the surgery for carpal & cubital tunnel in two weeks. Then I'll be ready to celebrate the holidays... lots to be thankful for this year!

A Milestone

November 9th, 2014.

Jim would have turned 60 years old today. His passing was more than 7 months ago. I still miss him and feel his presence all around me. He has inspired me so much these past few months as I read his journals and Mike and I share memories of him.

I had known Jim for several years. During the summer of 2013 we started seeing more of each other and became very close. I guess you could say I was his "last" girlfriend. We remained close until he passed away on March 28th. He took a piece of me with him when he left. But he also left me with so much more. I learned a lot from him and I am still learning even all these months later. He was such a complex guy and yet he wanted just one simple thing in life... a partner. Someone who understood him... who "got" him. After dating a few women half his age, he began to realize that he had met his match with me. Probably because I didn't let him get away with any crap.

During our short time together I felt that we were just getting to know and understand each other really well. We just ran out of time. He was very special and our connection was hard to figure out, even for us... but we knew there was significant meaning to it.

I know as these milestones come and go I will think of Jim and smile. It took me a long time to get to this point. I cried for months after he passed, even though I knew he wouldn't want me to be miserable in that way. Time is the great healer though. He changed my life and who I am. I feel like I am a better person for having known and loved him. I also know that we will meet again one day. That thought brings me the most comfort.

God Bless and keep you Jim... until we meet again.

At a party June 2013

It's a gusher!

November 12, 2014

Well, I've had an interesting morning. I saw the plastic surgeon yesterday and had my two little stitches removed. He said I could start using vitamin E oil on the scars if I wanted to and that everything looked really great.

This morning I got up and was rubbing the oil on the scars when the right one (formerly known as the "good" boob) let out a gush of blood! I was so stunned I couldn't believe it. I reached for a tissue and another gush of blood came out. The tissue lasted just long enough for me to get a washcloth. I had to hold it firmly against the incision to keep it from gushing while I called the doctor. They said to come in right away. I realized I couldn't drive myself and hold the compression so I did a quick mental check of who was available. I knew Bobbie, Dawn and Laura were all out of town, so I called my sister. She was able to come get me and run me over there.

Turns out it was a seroma. It wasn't exactly blood gushing out - it was blood plasma. This is not all that uncommon and since I did not have drains this time, the fluid pooled in the area and once the leak sprung, it just kept coming out. Kinda like that boy whose finger plugged up the dam!

So, they let it drain out as much as possible put a couple more stitches in and then glued me back together. I'm starting to feel like Humpty Dumpty here. I'll go back in a week to get the stitches out and have to take antibiotics just to be safe. I'm glad it wasn't really anything major but I think anyone would come "unglued" to see that much blood gushing out of their body!

I got the MRI yesterday and it doesn't show any masses behind the SC Joint. I am scheduled to get a steroid injection to help with the pain. I'm not sure if that's a temporary fix or what but it will be good to get some relief and hopefully the joint will heal itself. Next on the agenda is the carpal-cubital tunnel surgery, which will have my right arm in a sling for about two weeks. That will require some prepping the day before so I can manage as a lefty for a while.

That was enough excitement for one day. It's been cold and snowy anyway so I think a day of channel surfing is in order. That won't even be too exciting considering I only get about 4-5 channels!

One arm wonder

November 21, 2014

I had my carpal and cubital tunnel surgery done a few days ago, so I am writing this using the old "hunt-and-peck" method. This should only take an hour or so! I was hoping to get a "two-fer" on this surgery but I don't think they do that. Maybe I should have waited until Black Friday. It was a pretty simple surgery, compared to the others I've had. This is my sixth surgery in less than a year though so I think I am DONE!

I have a splint and a sling, which is about as big and heavy as the old plaster casts! Here I am waving hello.

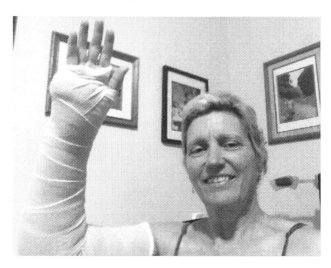

It took several hours before the nerve block wore off. That was really weird! I had a nerve block last year when I had the initial double mastectomy but it's very different when it's a limb. My arm hung there, useless and heavy. I was telling my fingers to move but they weren't listening! When I went to bed, I had pillows propped up all around me but that didn't stop my arm from falling one way or the other. I woke up a few times wondering where my arm was. I'm surprised I didn't knock myself upside the head! Sometime in the middle of the night I moved my fingers and touched my thumb to my index finger. By morning I was wiggling away! That was a relief!

Oh, and just to add a little complication to the surgery, they had to give me the IV in my foot! I can't have needle sticks or blood pressure in my left arm due to the lack of lymph nodes in the axillary area, which can cause lymphadema. So, IV in my right foot, blood pressure cuff on my left calf... problem solved! We managed to make the nurses laugh about it at least.

I think this last surgery was one of the most entertaining in that respect. The nurses would look at me when I told them about my left arm and then say "Let me think about this." Especially since I had to have those compression devices on my legs during the procedure. Then it was a matter of putting those on over or under the BP cuff. I used to be really simple and now I am so complicated! I hate when that happens.

So, I've been sitting around a lot the past few days. I was told not to do anything for at least three days. Today is the third day. I think tomorrow I will go do another 14er. Ha - just kidding. Wanted to see if you were paying attention!

I'll continue to take it slow. My mom and sister Cheryl are coming in for Thanksgiving so that will make the holiday even better! My sister Eva will cook up the turkey and some dressing and I'll be one happy camper!

My splint and dressing get to come off just before Thanksgiving so I can dig into the "other" dressing! I will see the doc for a follow up the following week and we'll go from there. I may be released to return to work in December but I have vacation to burn so I am hoping to be off through the year-end. I'm not sure I will still know how to do my job and I am not guaranteed my job will be there but I'm good with whatever happens. Again, that leap of faith I am facing.

I will be wrapping up my journal soon and have converted it to a book form. I hope to be published early in 2015.

I wish everyone a blessed Thanksgiving. I know I have much to be thankful for as this has been a year of giving and of thanks and gratitude like I've never known before.

God Bless

Not so fast there, missy!

November 24, 2014

If this past year hasn't been enough to give me an ulcer, wait until you hear this one! I just have to laugh whenever something seems amiss with my body anymore. And I certainly have to stop asking the question "What else could possibly happen?" It appears my body is taking that as a challenge.

After surgery on Tuesday I noticed my right eye was a little bloodshot. I read in the handout that the nerve block can cause headache, bloodshot eyes, etc so I didn't think much of it. By Thursday it was a little scratchy and by Friday it was hurting. I didn't sleep well Friday night so I called my Optometrist Saturday morning and got in to see him. He diagnosed it as Keratitis. He referred me to an Ophthalmologist but gave me drops that were a combo steroid and antibiotic to help over the weekend.

Meanwhile, I had an appointment with the Orthopedic Doc on Monday morning for a steroid injection for my SC Joint dislocation. I was a little anxious about it so I asked Bobbie to come with me. Even adults need a security blanket now and then! It actually went very well. It was kinda fun too as I checked in and seeing the confusion on faces since my arm is still in the splint and they show I am here for the shoulder! Even the doc gave me a questioned look when he came in!

So back to the Ophthalmologist… he says I have an ulcer on my cornea. He gave me drops to put in every hour today and come back again tomorrow. These are very powerful antibiotics and the hope is to speed the healing process. My cells must be as stubborn as I am… they always give me mega-antibiotics! Back for the follow up the next day and it was looking much better, so I'll continue the drops every 3-4 hours and go back next week. Hopefully that will be the end of that, but I guess that is yet to be "seen!"

All in all, I think things are winding down for the year and all of this "medical" stuff. I feel like it's time to wrap it up and bid farewell to all my doctor and nurse friends. My goal for the New Year is be to be strong and healthy and to enjoy life. What else is there really that's more important than that?

The End

Here's another fitting ending. Just for good measure I asked my General Practitioner to throw in a colonoscopy this year. Why not? That is truly a perfect ending!

I stopped in to get my prep kit and I have to hand it to them, they have a great sense of humor. They have the *Bottoms Up Café* on the premises for starters. They have t-shirts and other merchandise that says "Up Yours – and we mean that sincerely." I mean, you gotta love someone who can poke fun at what they do for a living!

# Reflection and Perception

It's Thanksgiving Day – November 27, 2014. I can't think of a more appropriate day to wrap up this story.

To say I have much to be thankful for this year is an understatement. A year of surgeries, chemo, illness and loss of a loved one doesn't seem like anything to be thankful for. But as I've said all along in this journey, in one short year I have learned the lessons of a lifetime. I am in a very different place in life than I was a year ago and it's a much better place. I have many people to thank for that.

Up until a few days ago I was very uncertain what my future holds. I am still not sure if I have a job to go back to but that will work itself out. I do know that I want to do something that brings me joy. I read a book recently that spoke of how we work at our jobs for years and years so that we can retire and do what we love. But what about doing what we love now?

I wasn't sure what I loved until recently and now it seems quite obvious to me. I enjoy hiking and being outdoors in Colorado. I love to explore and spend time with friends and experience all of the Lords amazing creations. I also discovered that I enjoy writing. Until I encountered Calypso, I didn't know what I had to write about so if I hadn't taken this journey I may not have had the chance to discover my voice. Journaling about this has been an amazing experience in itself. At first it was a means for me to write about how I was feeling and to keep friends and family informed of how things were going.

Somewhere along the way I discovered I enjoyed it and I was getting great feedback from friends and family about my writing. Thank you all who encouraged and supported me. That is how this book came to be and I hope to do more so I can see if I have "The Write Stuff!"

So, thanks to everyone that has been in my life and a part of this journey. No matter how big or small your part was, I hope you know it has lead me to a path that I look forward to more than any other in my life. Just like the trails that I spend so much time on, this new path will be much more enjoyable with the company of good friends. I hope you will continue to be a part of my life so we can make these new discoveries together.

Here's to a new life in 2015!

A final thought and a good reminder:

"We are not human beings going through a temporary spiritual experience. We are spiritual beings going through a temporary human experience."

Thank you – Thank you – Thank you!

Thank you to Laura Canini and Craig Highsmith for throwing several parties in my favor and helping me at home and accompanying me to chemo. And to my other chemo volunteers: Pam Ransom, Mary Charney, Connie Brown, Greg Gulfoil, Mike Ryan, Matt Duffy, and Amy Kopycinski.

Thanks to GiveForward.com and to my sister Eva Richardson for coordinating the fund-raiser to help with my medical bills.

And to all those who contributed… Kate & Rodger Adams, Debbie & Keith Axe, Melissa Grant, Darryl & Julie, Cheryl Janca, Julee Janca, Jen & Brad Christensen, Jason Wood & Amanda Cole, Will & Nancy Huang, Garth Powell, John Andrews, Laura Butler, Marie Staigle, Jeff Reimer, Linda Howard, Pam Ransom, Laura Parr, Chet Bressman, Russ Palmer, Ben Cila, Janet Ogata, Catherine Hopkins, Ivy Lui-Hawkins, Betty Hatter, Kenna Belmont, Rox Belmont, Amy Casella, Wayne & Judy Richardson, Barb Paquette, Jim & Janine Sledz, Louise Becker, Rachel Lewis, Dana Parvin, Pat Stephenson, Peter & Toni Reynolds, Dave & Donna Hanning, Jada, Sue Berger, Monte Lau, Patricia Shih, Joe & Patty Skupski, Jean Palmquist, Matt Duffy, Karen Lundgren, Linda McLees, Jamie Bennington, Linda & Bruce Kaufman, Danitza Ogle, Jackie Enge, Mary Janca, Diane Brunette, Christy Caver, Sylvia Martin, Michelle Roberts.

Thanks again to Dawn & Bobbie for holding the Jewelry Fund raiser to help with medical bills.

Thanks to Lolly's Locks for my first no-cost wig and to the American Cancer Society for the second wig.

Thanks to CaringBridge.com for giving me an outlet to journal and keep family and friends *abreast* of things.

Thanks to Good Wishes for the custom made no-cost scarf.

Thank you to the doctors, nurses and all the staff at Memorial Hospital Outpatient Infusion Lab and to the Inpatient team as well. I always felt I had the best care both during chemo and during my hospital stay.

And many, many thanks to all who supported me in so many ways… your notes, emails, texts, phone calls, cards and gifts and mostly your prayers made all of this possible. I would not be where I am right now without all of you. My deepest and most heartfelt thanks to you all!

I recently read that the three hardest things for a person to say are: I Love You, I'm Sorry and Help Me.

I have no problem at all saying "I Love You" to the folks who have been part of this journey with me. You all hold a special place in my heart.

I don't think I struggle too much with "I'm sorry" either. I might have a little trouble with "I'm wrong" but not I'm sorry.

"Help me" was a tough one. It was really hard for me to ask but my friends made it seem so much easier. There were many times that I didn't even have to ask. You all just did what needed to be done.